Varieties of Peripheral Growth Models

Towards a New Comparative Political Economy of Development

Elements in Development Economics

DOI: 10.1017/9781009546751
First published online: February 2026

Michael Schedelik
Goethe University Frankfurt

Christian May
University of Hildesheim

Andreas Nölke
Goethe University Frankfurt

Daniel Mertens
University of Osnabrück

Alexandre De Podestá Gomes
State University of Campinas

Tobias ten Brink
Constructor University, Bremen

Author for correspondence: Michael Schedelik, schedelik@em.uni-frankfurt.de

Abstract: This Element seeks to develop an empirical research agenda that explores the applicability of the growth model perspective in comparative political economy to emerging capitalist economies (ECEs). Such an approach emphasizes the variety of possible growth models and their implications for development, providing an alternative to universalizing economic models as prevalent in mainstream development discourse. Using national accounts data for several large ECEs in the period from 2001 to 2022, the authors first propose a typology of peripheral growth models with varying degrees of economic vulnerability. Most notably, they add an investment-led model to the prevalent juxtaposition of consumption-led and export-led growth models. Subsequently, they employ several case vignettes from Brazil, Indonesia, South Africa, Turkey, Thailand, and Vietnam to unpack the effects of volatile international interdependencies, such as commodity cycles, and diverse political underpinnings on peripheral growth models. This title is also available as open access on Cambridge Core.

Keywords: commodity price cycles, comparative political economy, economic vulnerability, growth models, development economics

© UNU-WIDER 2026

ISBNs: 9781009546737 (HB), 9781009546744 (PB), 9781009546751 (OC)
ISSNs: 2755-1601 (online), 2755-1598 (print)

Contents

1 Introduction: Peripheral Growth Models and Economic Development   1

2 Theory and Framework   7

3 A Typology of Peripheral Growth Models   17

4 International Interdependencies and Peripheral Growth Models   29

5 The Political Underpinnings of Peripheral Growth Models   45

6 Conclusion and Perspectives   60

References   64

Elements in Development Economics
Series Editor-in-Chief
Kunal Sen
UNU-WIDER and University of Manchester

VARIETIES OF PERIPHERAL GROWTH MODELS

Towards a New Comparative Political Economy of Development

Michael Schedelik
Goethe University Frankfurt

Christian May
University of Hildesheim

Andreas Nölke
Goethe University Frankfurt

Daniel Mertens
University of Osnabrück

Alexandre De Podestá Gomes
State University of Campinas

Tobias ten Brink
Constructor University, Bremen

Shaftesbury Road, Cambridge CB2 8EA, United Kingdom

One Liberty Plaza, 20th Floor, New York, NY 10006, USA

477 Williamstown Road, Port Melbourne, VIC 3207, Australia

314–321, 3rd Floor, Plot 3, Splendor Forum, Jasola District Centre, New Delhi – 110025, India

Cambridge University Press is part of Cambridge University Press & Assessment, a department of the University of Cambridge.

We share the University's mission to contribute to society through the pursuit of education, learning, and research at the highest international levels of excellence.

www.cambridge.org
Information on this title: www.cambridge.org/9781009546737
DOI: 10.1017/9781009546751

© UNU-WIDER 2026

This publication is in copyright. Subject to statutory exception and to the provisions of relevant collective licensing agreements, with the exception of the Creative Commons version the link for which is provided below, no reproduction of any part may take place without the written permission of Cambridge University Press & Assessment.

An online version of this work is published at doi.org/10.1017/9781009546751 under a Creative Commons Open Access license CC-BY-NC-SA 3.0 IGO which permits re-use, distribution, and reproduction in any medium for non-commercial purposes providing appropriate credit to the original work is given, any changes made are indicated, and the new work is published under the same licence terms. When the licensor is an intergovernmental organisation, disputes will be resolved by mediation and arbitration where possible. To view a copy of this license, visit https://creativecommons.org/licenses/by-nc-sa/3.0/igo

When citing this work, please include a reference to the DOI 10.1017/9781009546751

First published 2026

A catalogue record for this publication is available from the British Library

ISBN 978-1-009-54673-7 Hardback
ISBN 978-1-009-54674-4 Paperback
ISSN 2755-1601 (online)
ISSN 2755-1598 (print)

Cambridge University Press & Assessment has no responsibility for the persistence or accuracy of URLs for external or third-party internet websites referred to in this publication and does not guarantee that any content on such websites is, or will remain, accurate or appropriate.

For EU product safety concerns, contact us at Calle de José Abascal, 56, 1°, 28003 Madrid, Spain, or email eugpsr@cambridge.org

1 Introduction: Peripheral Growth Models and Economic Development

Few debates in development studies are as contentious as the one over the sources of development and growth. A wide range of competing growth theories is available – both neoclassical and heterodox (see Jones & Vollrath, 2013; Aghion & Howitt, 2009 for the former, and Hein, 2014; Blecker & Setterfield, 2019 for the latter). Yet, the fact that only a small number of economies have successfully caught up with advanced countries since the second half of the twentieth century has only intensified the growth debate, especially in light of rising global inequalities since the 1980s and the stagnation of once rapidly growing late developers (Johnson & Papageorgiou, 2020). This discussion is particularly critical for peripheral economies, where challenges such as absolute poverty, lack of social safety nets, health crises, and – increasingly – climate vulnerability are sorely felt. In response, a range of scholarly approaches have tried to shed new light on the enduring questions of growth and development in global capitalism (e.g., Banerjee & Duflo, 2019; Mazzucato, 2023; Sen, 2023; Rodrik & Stiglitz, 2024; Acemoglu, 2025; Rodrik, 2025).

In recent decades, the debate on the political economy of development has arguably been shaped by the grand theories of new institutional economics and the developmental state (Acemoglu & Robinson, 2012; Haggard, 2018; see Section 2.1). Both focus on the necessary conditions for the successful transition to a high-income economy, deriving insights about this process from a few selected countries that achieved this goal. The debate has too often focused on individual "role models" for catch-up development – most notably South Korea – (see, e.g., Lee, 2013), tending to downplay the structural conditions of the vast majority of developing and emerging economies that need to get into a growth-enabling phase in the first place. While we are far from denying the importance of institutions and state bureaucracies for economic and political development, this Element proposes a different perspective for the study of growth trajectories in so-called emerging economies such as Brazil, Indonesia, South Africa, Thailand, or Turkey. Starting from the observation that growth in these economies mostly occurs in episodes that are characterized by volatility, shaped by pronounced boom-bust cycles and sustained phases of stagnation (Pritchett et al., 2017), we introduce the *growth model perspective* to development studies. We contend that this middle-range theory helps explain why some countries succeed in pursuing sustained periods of economic growth and stabilizing a highly volatile growth trajectory, while others fail and experience major crises and periods of stagnation. Thus, our claim is rather narrow: Instead of projecting long-term catch-up development to high-income status, the approach proposed here allows for examining growth dynamics in a shorter time frame, accounting for incremental changes in varying growth trajectories.

Developed simultaneously in post-Keynesian economics (PKE) and comparative political economy (CPE), the growth model perspective analyzes advanced capitalist economies by unpacking their aggregate demand composition and respective political underpinnings (e.g., Baccaro & Pontusson, 2016, 2018; Hein et al., 2021; Hassel & Palier, 2021; Stockhammer, 2022; Kohler & Stockhammer, 2022; Baccaro et al., 2022). Growth models in these research traditions are understood through an empirical-historical lens, aiming to establish Weberian ideal types to allow for context-sensitive, mid-level theorizing on the similarities and differences of capitalist economies and their trajectories of expansion, stagnation, crisis, and change. More specifically, Baccaro and Pontusson (2016) traced the emergence of two interdependent types of growth models in countries belonging to the Organisation for Economic Co-operation and Development (OECD): a consumption-led growth model, partly bolstering domestic demand through household debt, and an export-led growth model, replacing domestic with external demand. Their intervention triggered an ongoing debate about the relative importance of demand-side and supply-side factors for growth (see Hope & Soskice, 2016; Hassel & Palier, 2021; Schedelik et al., 2021; Stockhammer, 2022), reflecting a renewed interest among political economists in macroeconomics and its relation to politics (Amable et al., 2019; Baccaro & Pontusson, 2018; Blyth & Matthijs, 2017; Schwartz & Tranøy, 2019). Subsequently, the growth model (GM) perspective has been used to explain international economic imbalances (e.g., De Ville & Vermeiren, 2016; Johnston & Regan, 2016; Hall, 2018; Akcay et al., 2022) and to map out the variety of growth models in advanced capitalist economies (Hein et al., 2021; Picot, 2021).

By introducing the growth model perspective to the broader field of development studies and applying the perspective to peripheral economies in global capitalism, this Element pursues two major goals. The first goal is to instigate a conversation between different research communities, in order to advance the debate on the sources and politics of development and growth (Acemoglu & Robinson, 2012; Pritchett et al., 2017; Kelsall et al., 2022; Behuria, 2025). While the GM perspective is most vibrantly debated in CPE, an established interdisciplinary literature rooted in political science, sociology, and (heterodox) economics, broader questions of development and change – especially in non-OECD countries – are usually dealt with in the cross-disciplinary field of development studies. Despite occasional interactions in the past (e.g., Evans & Stephens, 1988), there are few interactions or conceptual overlaps found today. We believe that this separation has produced shortcomings. Among them is the tendency in development economics to emphasize stylized universal growth trajectories that every country will eventually follow, as was already common in, for example, Lewis (1954) or Rostow (1960). The basic assumption in this latter tradition holds that countries can be treated symmetrically and that their long-term growth trajectories follow more or less the same patterns (but see Sen 2023 for an accommodating approach). In neo-institutionalist economics, the precondition to achieve higher rates of economic growth is strong institutions, associated with property rights, the rule of law, and liberal democracy. The developmental state approach sees state capacity as the main solution for the intricate problems of growth. The literature in CPE has rejected such perspectives and, by contrast, focuses on the persistent divergence of development paths and major differences in policy responses to external shocks. It seeks to explain these differences with the help of typological theories of capitalist economies (Clift, 2021; May et al., 2024) and emphasizes diverse, uneven, and interdependent growth trajectories in a global economy. Leveraging the typological approach common in CPE, we believe, can help move beyond a one-size-fits-all perspective and provide new ground for conversation. In other words, having this conversation may contribute to understanding some of the enduring and intricate puzzles of development studies, especially why some countries thrive within imperfect economic and institutional conditions.

The second goal this Element pursues is to advance the growth model perspective in CPE itself, by adapting its concepts to countries beyond the well-studied hemisphere of OECD economies. Moving beyond the existing geographical confines of the GM perspective means exploring its applicability to so-called emerging capitalist economies (ECEs). ECEs are conventionally understood as countries transitioning from low-income, low-productivity economies with informal institutions toward higher-income economies, with expanding domestic markets and an accommodating set of institutions in financial systems, property rights, and industrial organization. Brazil, China, Mexico, Thailand, and Turkey are just a few of the countries in this heterogeneous group. The term emerging capitalist economies has become standard in the field, so we adhere to this convention. However, this does not imply agreement with the implicit normative assumption that every ECE will inevitably grow and develop – emerge – by further integrating into the global economy and strengthening capitalist institutions. On the contrary, instances of earlier successful catch-up are relatively rare. Many ECEs tend to experience severe growth slowdowns and periods of stagnation. In fact, as we argue in this Element, the particular way in which many ECEs are integrated into the global economy makes their development trajectories especially vulnerable to the whims of international capital. We therefore analyze their growth trajectories in terms of *peripheral growth models*, based on a recent cross-fertilization between the GM perspective and dependency approaches (Madariaga & Palestini, 2021; Schedelik et al., 2021, 2023; Avlijas & Gartzou-Katsouyanni, 2024, 2025; Bulfone et al., 2025). One important advantage of this cross-fertilization is that it bases the study of economic growth in part on a perspective born from the periphery, thereby challenging the usual application of models developed in and for the global North to the global South. Moreover, economic dependencies today are not only pronounced in North-South relationships but also increasingly matter in relations between China and other countries of the South (Stallings, 2022). Finally, the combination of the GM perspective with dependency approaches also addresses a typical problem inherent in contemporary versions of the latter, such as the discussion on international financial subordination (Kvangraven et al., 2021; Alami et al., 2023). Such a combination assists in balancing the structuralist bias of dependency theory with the potential for economic agency highlighted by the GM perspective (Petry & Nölke, 2025; Schedelik & Nölke, 2025).

From our point of view, it is overdue to extend the GM perspective to this group of countries. After all, an approach centered on "growth" should provide meaningful insights about actually growing economies, which are increasingly to be found outside of the OECD. This shift in the global distribution of economic growth started in the early 1990s and is often attributed to the rise of China and the BRICS[1] on the one hand and the exhaustion of the postwar growth regime in the "West" on the other (Blyth & Matthjis, 2017). Consequently, the center of growth in the global economy has moved in the last decades: Around 2008, for the first time, more than half of global GDP was accounted for by developing and emerging economies (Figure 1).

Overall, however, growth trajectories of developing and emerging economies are significantly different from those of advanced economies. Whereas the latter typically are characterized by a relatively stable long-run average growth rate, the former are characterized by higher volatility. This manifests itself in a stop-and-go pattern of growth, that is, sudden shifts between growth accelerations, slowdowns, and even outright collapses (Jones & Olken, 2008; Kar et al., 2013). Hence, peripheral growth models in ECEs tend to show higher degrees of vulnerability, defined traditionally as "the exposure to external shocks" (Briguglio et al., 2009, 229; see Figure 2). A large part of this vulnerability stems from the external sector of these economies and relates to volatile export revenues, typically in a handful of commodities, as well as volatile capital flows, both portfolio and foreign direct investment flows. While these factors

---

[1] Brazil, Russia, India, China, and South Africa.

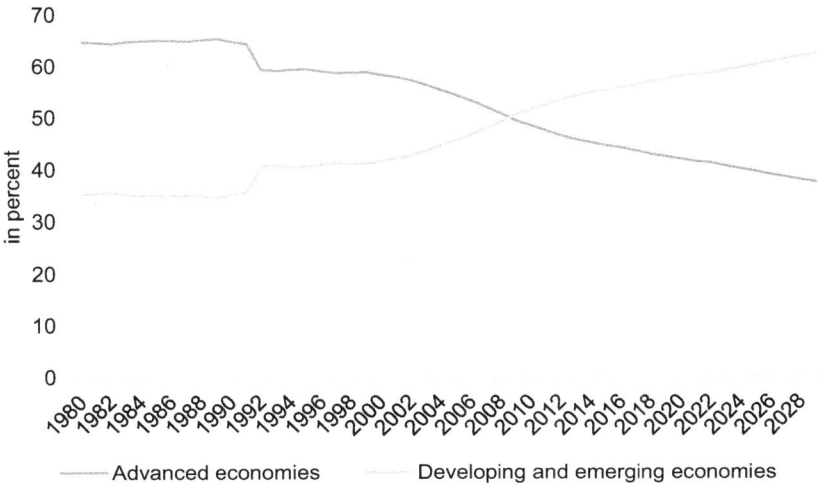

Figure 1 GDP based on purchasing power parity (PPP), share of world GDP, 1980–2028

Source: IMF, World Economic Outlook database, estimates from 2025 onwards

on their own are well researched, they are not yet integrated into an encompassing theoretical framework of growth. By advancing the GM perspective for the study of emerging economies, we aim to provide such a framework.

Our framework to study *peripheral growth models* builds on three pillars: (1) a novel and coherent typology of growth models in emerging economies, which highlights (2) different modes of integration into global economic structures and processes that lead to varying degrees of macroeconomic vulnerabilities. These vulnerabilities, in turn, can potentially be mitigated by (3) economic policies, broad political coalitions, and coordinated state-business relations that are specific to the political economy of peripheral growth models – and which are often better understood by scholars of development. Here again, by adapting the toolbox of growth model research to ECEs, we hope to spark greater cross-disciplinary and global engagement.

Against this backdrop, this Element is structured as follows: Section 2 reviews the main theoretical approaches to economic growth and development in various literatures in political economy and development studies. Based on this discussion, we introduce our own analytical framework for the study of peripheral growth models and present the methodological approach used in this Element. Section 3 proposes a typology of peripheral growth models and employs national accounts data to identify growth models in large ECEs over the past twenty years. Based on this descriptive dataset, it elaborates on the

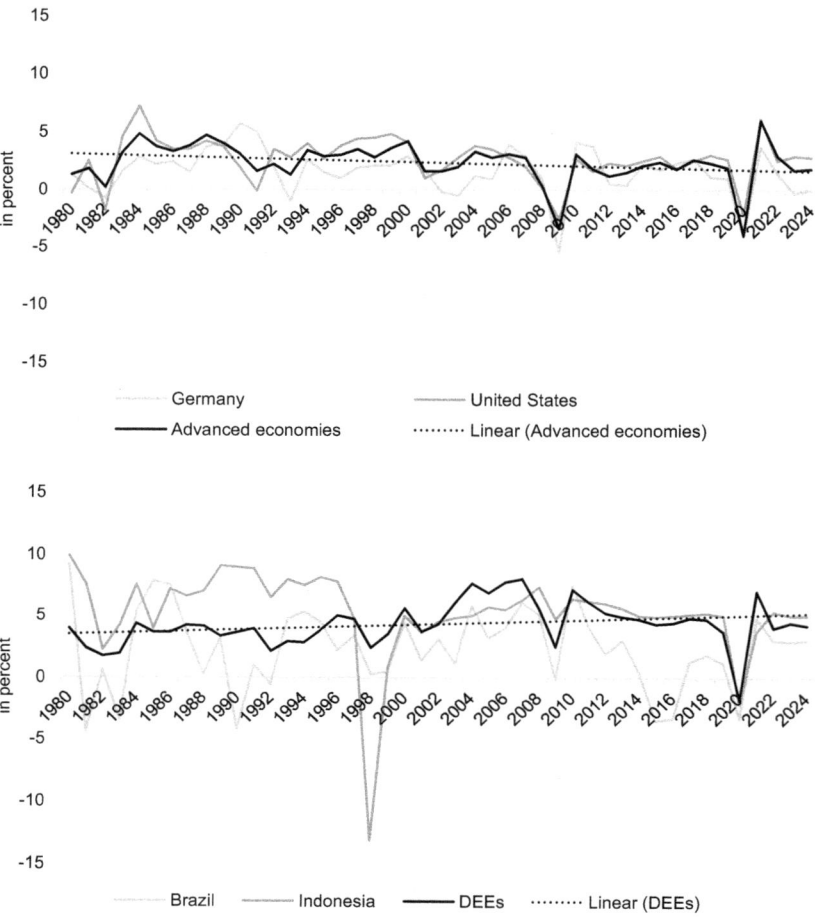

Figure 2 Annual real GDP growth of selected countries and country aggregates[2]

Source: IMF, World Economic Outlook database

relevance and vulnerabilities of an "investment-led growth model," which has so far received insufficient attention in the GM perspective. The section then lays out the small-N case universe from which we draw subsequent illustrative vignettes. Section 4 highlights how peripheral growth models are shaped through international interdependencies by analyzing the effects of global commodity cycles on the growth experience of several major exporters of primary resources, exemplified by Brazil and Indonesia, during and after the recent commodity boom. We further elaborate on the effects of global financial

---

[2] DEE denotes: developing and emerging economies.

cycles on emerging countries, particularly those pursuing debt-based growth models, such as South Africa and Turkey. We finally point to the role of global value chains (GVCs) and foreign direct investment (FDI) for the investment-led growth models of countries such as Thailand and Vietnam in Southeast Asia. Subsequently, Section 5 analyzes the interaction of growth models and political dynamics in non-Western political settings by reflecting on the political support for growth models of selected emerging economies. Lastly, Section 6 concludes with a summary of the results, discussing the policy implications and future research avenues for the GM perspective in particular and the political economy of development more broadly.

2 Theory and Framework

In this section, we first review several theoretical approaches to economic development at the intersection of political science, sociology, and economics. Highlighting strengths and weaknesses of these perspectives, we argue for moving beyond the established fault lines in the development discourse. We do this by advancing the growth model perspective in CPE for the study of growth trajectories in emerging economies. Therefore, we subsequently introduce the main theoretical debate in CPE between the varieties of capitalism (VoC) approach and the GM perspective, arguing for an accommodating approach. We then propose our conceptual framework of *peripheral growth models,* which builds on but significantly extends traditional GM analyses. Finally, we discuss the case selection and research design for the empirical sections of this Element.

2.1 Political Economy Approaches to Economic Development

The neo-institutionalist literature in economics has revived the debate about the causes of (under)development (North, 1995; Greif, 2006; Acemoglu & Robinson, 2012). This approach contends that strong institutions tend to achieve higher rates of economic development because these institutions provide the necessary incentives for investment, innovation, human capital accumulation, and economic exchange. By now, there is an established consensus that "institutions matter" for long-term growth (Rodrik et al., 2004; Acemoglu et al., 2005). Though disagreement persists over what the best institutional design looks like, the dominant view has it that liberal political and economic institutions trump all other arrangements. Daron Acemoglu and James Robinson have advanced this perspective in their account on "why nations fail" (Acemoglu & Robinson, 2012). According to them, "inclusive" political and economic institutions associated with free markets, property rights, the rule of law, and pluralist democracy are prerequisites for economic growth. "Extractive" institutions divert resources away from their most efficient and socially optimal use by powerful elites. In a nutshell, Acemoglu and Robinson's approach arguably proposes one universally applicable model for development: The liberal market economy, which is enforced and sustained by liberal democracy, thereby disavowing or even denying indigenous institutional constellations (Madra et al., 2025, 7–8).

The neo-institutionalist approach has encountered severe criticism, however. To begin with, the dichotomy of inclusive and exclusive institutions is too simple to capture the real-world variety of institutional arrangements, their historical origins, and embeddedness in a hierarchically structured, globalized economy (Chang, 2011; Ince, 2024). Furthermore, this perspective, focusing on long-run growth rates, fails to explain the volatile growth episodes so prevalent in emerging economies (Pritchett et al., 2017, 12). Finally, such a perspective cannot explain why many countries industrialized under authoritarian rule with heavy state intervention – the most obvious contemporary examples being East Asian "developmental states" and, more recently, China (Sen et al., 2018; ten Brink, 2019). At the very least, an endorsement of these facts calls for more nuanced, context-sensitive institutional analyses devoted to mid-level theorizing (Merton, 1968), rejecting universally valid one-size-fits-all accounts.

The developmental state literature mentioned earlier is one major example of a deep engagement with country case studies and comparative historical analysis (Johnson, 1982; Amsden, 1989; Wade, 1990; Evans, 1995). Primarily occupied with explaining the growth miracles of first- and second-tier East Asian late industrializers, this literature has informed a broad and lively debate about the role of the state in economic development (Rodrik, 2009; Stiglitz & Lin, 2013). After the 2008 financial crisis, this discussion has gained considerable momentum even in OECD countries (Mazzucato, 2013; Breznitz & Gingrich, 2025). However, given the peculiarities of the East Asian developmental states and the specific external conditions permissive of their export-led growth models (Haggard, 2019, 54–9), Johnson (1982, 307) warned early on: "the dangers of institutional abstraction are as great as the potential advantages" of adopting Japan's growth strategy in other contexts. Hence, the "quest for capacious and strategically oriented state institutions has ultimately proved elusive," as only a handful of countries have achieved such a high degree of state capacity (Naseemullah, 2023, 7). Over time, the notion of developmental state has become a rather abstract buzzword detached from its origins and main conceptual elements (Fine, 2013). Accordingly, the debate has shifted toward new directions, such as the question of whether a capacious state bureaucracy is possible at all in times of financialization and neoliberalism (Evans & Heller, 2015; Fine & Pollen, 2018).

Hence, both neo-institutionalist and developmental state approaches tend to imply a (normative) linear model of development, which countries would only need to apply fully in order to achieve high levels of economic growth. Furthermore, development is treated as a purely domestic process, which, in our view, underestimates the structural conditions of the global political economy. Both approaches usually highlight the flaws of development in different countries, as the record of successful adopters of either model is quite small. In particular, Korea and Taiwan are seen as role models for development, successfully transitioning from a low- to high-income status in the twentieth century. However, these cases are economies with particular geopolitical and historical-institutional legacies, making it hard to generalize their developmental state model globally (Naseemullah, 2023). In addition, these countries recorded robust export growth throughout a large part of their development trajectory, highlighting the particular global economic conditions of the second half of the twentieth century in which they could grow through such a model. These structural conditions of the global political economy, so we contend, have changed in such a fundamental way that it is impossible to directly compare the growth trajectories of the 1960s and 1970s with those of the 2000s and onward.

This argument has also been highlighted by approaches that explain growth and development exogenously, locating the sources of and conditions for (under)development at the level of the global political economy. Drawing on dependency theory, world systems, postcolonial, and other critical approaches (e.g., Cardoso & Faletto, 1979; Wallerstein, 1976), this important strand of research investigates the hierarchical structure of the global economy and its constraining impact on economic development in peripheral countries. Contemporary versions of this argument underline three aspects of today's global capitalism: global commodity markets, financial flow cycles, and global production networks. Studies on global commodity markets highlight the dependence of many developing and emerging economies on exporting commodities. These dependencies are profound, given the cyclical nature of commodity price movements over time (Akyüz, 2022; Schedelik et al., 2023). Similarly, scholars working on "dependent" or "subordinate" financialization highlight the severe repercussions of short-term financial flows on these economies (Bonizzi et al., 2022; Lapavitsas & Soydan, 2022). Finally, the literature on global production networks argues that developing countries often are integrated in a subordinate position in these networks, being responsible for low-tech production, low-skills employment, harsh working conditions, and profound pollution (Wang et al., 2021). In all of these regards, the fate of peripheral economies is perceived as more or less determined by the overwhelming forces of the global economy, leaving little room for economic agency (Petry & Nölke, 2025; Schedelik & Nölke, 2025; on this see also Avlijaš & Gartzou-Katsouyanni, 2024, 2025).

All exogenous–focused approaches arguably suffer from an underestimation of domestic politics beyond elites and state bureaucracies. This shortcoming has been addressed by the political settlements analysis approach (Khan, 2000, 2010). It emphasizes how the distribution of power in society, including formal institutions but also informal networks and patron-client relations, can support or thwart developmental goals. Particularly in developing economies, where the economic structure is dominated by primary commodities, there is a need to promote economic diversification and technological upgrading. Contrary to the dominant neo-institutionalist view, certain types of rents can contribute positively to development. In this context, rents are broadly understood as "excess incomes, which do not exist in perfect markets" (Khan, 2000, 21). "Rents for learning" and "Schumpeterian rents," which are necessary for the promotion of economic diversification, indigenous technological capabilities, and innovation, do not necessarily equate with waste and inefficiencies. As long as the distribution of power allows those rents to be used productively, state capture can be avoided. Traditionally, the political settlements literature lends itself to detailed country case studies, but recent endeavors have also tried to build a more quantitative approach (Kelsall et al., 2022; for a recent review, see Behuria, 2025).

By employing the growth model approach for developing and emerging economies, we aim to offer an alternative route mediating between the grand theories of neo-institutionalism, developmental state, and dependency. The growth model perspective is both more pragmatic and realist: It is pragmatic because it accounts for the incremental improvements of growth-enabling institutions and policies, knowing that hardly any country can "imitate" the trajectories of Korea, Taiwan, or – nowadays – China. It is realist in the sense that it treats development conditions as they are, not as they should be. Crucially, this entails that the task of development is first and foremost to minimize vulnerability, which is the major factor for stagnant or negative growth in the first place.

To summarize, existing political economy approaches to economic development have considerable strengths, but also major shortcomings. Regarding the latter, a preference for universally valid one-size-fits-all accounts seems to be the most prominent one. This is not only a problem for large parts of the neo-institutionalist literature, but also for part of the developmental state discussion, which tends to abstract from the particular circumstances of the East Asian cases during the mid twentieth century. Moreover, the recent rejuvenation of dependency approaches thus far tends to underplay the economic agency of emerging economies. Against this backdrop, typological approaches in CPE have the potential to complement existing perspectives on development by highlighting opportunities for macroeconomic agency in a context-sensitive way.

2.2 Approaches in Comparative Political Economy: Varieties of Capitalism and Growth Models

In contrast to the neo-institutionalist focus on a narrow set of institutions (e.g., property rights and the rule of law), CPE approaches build on a much richer set of socioeconomic institutions that account for the multidimensionality of growth trajectories. Along with regulation theory and the national business systems approach, particularly the VoC paradigm has been a key reference point in the CPE literature. This scholarship generally assumes that country-specific institutions matter for economic performance and that different institutional configurations are conducive to achieving economic and social objectives. Institutions are understood in a pragmatic way as solutions for coordination problems of firms. More specifically, it argues that key institutional spheres (such as corporate governance, financial system, industrial relations, or education and training), the identification of cross-cutting coordination mechanisms (inter-firm networks and associations versus competitive markets and formal contracts), as well as the notion of (positive) complementarities among institutions, allow for a parsimonious analysis of capitalist systems.

Crucially, VoC scholarship introduced ideal types of capitalist economies as analytical tools. Drawing on a long-established research tradition (Shonfield, 1965; Streeck, 2010, 6–15), Peter Hall and David Soskice made the now-classical distinction between liberal market economies and coordinated market economies (Hall & Soskice, 2001, 8). In the former, firms coordinate themselves primarily through competitive markets and formal contracts, whereas in the latter, they rely principally on inter-firm networks and associations. In contrast to the convergence thesis predominant in the 1990s, claiming that all capitalist economies would adapt themselves to the "superior" Anglo-Saxon model (Streeck 2010, 15–7), VoC argues that both types can be economically successful and internationally competitive, even in the long run. This idea rests on Hall and Soskice's notion of "comparative institutional advantage," which states that "the institutional structure of a particular political economy provides firms with advantages for engaging in specific types of activities there" (Hall &

Soskice, 2001, 37). As it does not focus on absolute, but comparative institutional advantages of nations, it is able to account for cross-national variation in product specialization.

Recent research has extended the VoC perspective, identifying four main types of emerging market capitalism (Schedelik et al., 2021; Friel, 2024): (1) a dependent market economy, originally envisaged for Central and Eastern Europe (Nölke & Vliegenthart, 2009); (2) a hierarchical market economy, modelled after Latin American economies (Schneider, 2013), but also identified in Turkey (Kiran, 2018); (3) a state-permeated market economy, found in East Asia (Carney, 2016), China (ten Brink, 2019), India and temporarily in Brazil (Nölke et al., 2020); and (4) a patrimonial market economy (Becker, 2013), as depicted for the Arab world (Schlumberger, 2008) as well as for Russia and other former Soviet countries (Becker & Vasileva, 2017). Focusing on supply-side institutions and firm characteristics, the VoC research program, however, has largely tended to ignore three major points: demand-side macroeconomics, (distributive) politics, and a country's insertion in the global economy.[3] These points relate to the source and composition of economic growth (both domestic and external) as well as its stability through (domestic) political support and international factors such as financial flows or commodity price movements (Nölke et al., 2022; Schedelik et al., 2023). Since growth trajectories in emerging economies are more vulnerable and volatile than in advanced ones, these points are key for the purpose of this Element.

The GM perspective provided a response to the shortcomings of the VoC approach. It argues that national economies grow based on distinct patterns of demand (Baccaro & Pontusson 2016; Baccaro et al., 2022). Instead of focusing on institutions and firm-based production systems, this perspective emphasizes how economies generate and sustain demand to fuel growth. Growth models in this perspective are defined descriptively based on the decomposition of GDP growth and the respective leading demand components, differentiating between consumption-led (e.g., the UK) and export-led models (e.g., Germany), for instance (Baccaro et al., 2022). Crucially, the GM approach argues that such growth models are – to some degree – politically constructed and maintained. Governments shape particular models through their political choices and the respective macroeconomic policies. Business groups, unions, and voter segments form coalitions to support or contest a given model. Some GM analyses have used the Gramscian-inspired concept of a dominant social bloc to denote the political constellations of an entrenched bipartisan consensus on a growth strategy and crucial economic policies (Akcay & Jungmann, 2023; Apaydin,

---

[3] Except for the state-permeated type, see Nölke et al. (2020).

2025; on the social bloc concept, see Amable & Palombarini, 2024). The social bloc concept points to the occasional ideological framing of growth models as being in the "national interest," downplaying the interests of marginalized groups and the inherent contradictions of a particular model (May et al., 2024). At the same time, growth models are inherently unstable and can be disrupted by external shocks (like financial crises), internal contradictions (like rising inequality), or political shifts, leading to pressures for adjustment or transformation. To summarize, the GM perspective makes crisis and change central to understanding capitalist diversity. Comparative political economists using this lens study how and why countries adopt certain growth models, how they cope with crises, and how institutions, coalitions, and ideas help sustain or shift these models over time (Baccaro et al., 2022).[4]

2.3 Conceptual Framework: Peripheral Growth Models in Emerging Capitalist Economies

By looking at the components and drivers of economic growth, its distributional implications and political underpinnings, the GM research program has shifted scholarly attention from the institutional structures of capitalist economies and their supply side effects on growth – the focus of the VoC perspective – back to macroeconomics and aggregate demand (Schwartz & Tranøy, 2019). The analytical shift from supply to demand-side factors of the economy coincided with an evolving debate about the adequate macroeconomic theoretical foundations of growth model-inspired analyses (Hope & Soskice, 2016; Baccaro & Pontusson, 2018; Stockhammer, 2022). This discussion has led to substantial engagement of CPE scholars with PKE and its focus on "demand" or "growth regimes" (see Stockhammer, 2022: 164–170 for overviews).[5]

Although most growth model research to date has focused on advanced capitalist economies, first inroads have been made with regard to emerging economies (Schedelik et al., 2021; Wood & Schnyder, 2021; Akcay et al., 2022; Stockhammer, 2022; Jungmann, 2023; Baccaro & Hadziabdic, 2024; Campana et al., 2024; Bulfone et al., 2025). Country case studies and paired comparisons

---

[4] Within the context of development studies, one shortcoming of employing both VoC and the GM perspective is their narrow focus on economic performance and their reproduction of the growth paradigm (Green, 2022). In this sense, their application limits alternative understandings of development that are more reflective of other indicators of well-being or human-nature relations (see e.g., Alenda-Demoutiez, 2022).

[5] As the growth model research program in CPE (and parts of PKE) is confined to identifying 'growth models' (in the narrow sense) and their interplay with politics and institutions in national political economies, we do not factor in the vast PKE literature on 'demand regimes' in emerging economies, that is, studies estimating the effects of distributional changes on overall demand, its components and on economic growth (see Akcay et al., 2022).

have used the framework to analyze stability and change in emerging capitalist economies (e.g., Morgan et al., 2021; Nölke et al., 2022; Apaydin, 2025; Güngen & Akcay, 2024; Kalanta, 2024) while others have leveraged the economies of Central and Eastern Europe to explore the political economy of FDI-led growth (Avlijaš et al., 2021; Ban & Adascalitei, 2022; Bohle & Regan, 2021). Akcay et al. (2022), Campana et al. (2024), and Baccaro and Hadziabdic (2024) mapped the growth models of several large emerging economies and revealed not only variation between the countries but also a temporal shift in their growth models after the global financial crisis of 2008 and the end of the commodity boom in 2011 onward. Furthermore, recent scholarship has begun to conceptualize the notion of *peripheral growth models* (Stockhammer, 2023; Bulfone et al., 2025; Schedelik & Nölke, 2025), which refers to the "structural constraints imposed by global economic hierarchies" on growth trajectories in developing and emerging economies (Bulfone et al., 2025, 296).

These and other studies on the political economy of emerging capitalist economies have suggested several factors that fundamentally enhance our understanding of growth, stagnation, and crisis in these countries. These factors, we argue, need to be more systematically integrated into the empirical GM research program. This Element aims to do so with respect to what we think are the three most important factors that have to be reflected in the study of peripheral growth models in emerging economies:

(1) A coherent *typology of peripheral growth models* needs to be developed. Such a typology must go beyond OECD-centric views and needs to take into account the stronger role for investments in emerging economies, which results from the need to expand less developed infrastructure and productive capacities. In particular, an investment-led model needs to be added to the prevalent juxtaposition of consumption-led and export-led growth models.

(2) The *international context* is important in a different way for most ECEs than for advanced economies. Growth in ECEs depends more strongly on how the country is integrated into global economic hierarchies and on systemic dynamics that come in the form of commodity cycles (which undergird many export-led growth models), a dependency on foreign capital (e.g., via FDI), and through processes of financial subordination magnified by global financial cycles. These international interdependencies create profound vulnerabilities vis-à-vis external shocks, which are typical for peripheral growth models.

(3) Growth and stagnation in ECEs depend differently on the *embeddedness of economic actors in the political sphere* than in advanced economies. While

political coalitions and state-business relations are likely to define growth models across all types of political economies, the mechanisms through which politics shape particular growth trajectories in ECEs will usually differ from relatively stable Western systems of liberal democracy.

The selection of these factors is based on the literature on the political economy of development during the last decades. Based on this research, we are suggesting a more comprehensive research program for the GM perspective in emerging capitalist economies that not only studies macro-economic growth contributions in terms of aggregate demand components, but also systematically reflects on their international and macro-political embeddedness.[6] More specifically, we argue that, depending on the drivers of economic growth, a peripheral growth model's vulnerability vis-à-vis external shocks varies considerably. But as growth models do not emerge automatically, their nature and degree of vulnerability are subject to various political factors.

2.4 Case Selection and Methods

This Element investigates the growth trajectories of emerging capitalist economies, that is, mainly middle-income countries as defined by the World Bank. Our sample comprises thirteen ECEs that belong to the largest thirty-three countries with the biggest proportion of global GDP, according to the IMF (Table 1). This is where a large part of global growth has been attributed to, based on purchasing power parities. Given the GM perspective's (narrow) focus on analyzing growth trajectories, we use this metric for our case selection instead of GDP per capita. In addition, we also do not aim to account for catch-up processes and the transition from middle- to high-income status. This would require an ordering of countries according to certain income thresholds, usually defined in per capita terms. Finally, the countries in our sample are a very diverse set of economies with different political-economic regimes and historical-institutional legacies, covering all the major world regions. This, we contend, should assist us in developing our theoretical perspective of *peripheral growth models* as a useful and adaptive framework for the analysis of growth trajectories in emerging economies.

Methodologically, we are using the following approaches for tackling the identification of growth models in ECEs and macro-political factors. For the detection of peripheral growth models, we employ a simple demand-side approach for growth accounting, whereas our study of political factors sustaining these models will be based on country vignettes. Vignettes, which have

---

[6] More references to the relevant literature on the political economy of emerging economies are provided in the sections below.

Table 1 Selected indicators for the sample of emerging capitalist economies, 2024

Country	GDP, in billion US$ PPP	Rank
China	37,072,086	1
India	16,019,97	3
Russia	6,909,381	4
Brazil	4,702,004	7
Indonesia	4,658,321	8
Turkey	3,456,771	12
Mexico	3,303,067	13
Egypt	2,231,822	17
Thailand	1,771,532	22
Vietnam	1,631,796	25
Nigeria	1,489,832	27
Argentina	1,353,804	31
South Africa	993,745	33

Source: IMF, World Economic Outlook database

found their way from social psychology into other social sciences, are commonly understood to present case histories for the purpose of illustrating important traits of a situation or constellation. Importantly, they lend themselves particularly well to the development of a research program, in comparison to other traditions of case study research that require thick descriptions (Hughes, 1998, 381; Welch et al., 2011, 751–2).

Our vignettes are short case studies on the political factors supporting specific growth models. They do not claim to provide comprehensive evidence, but rather to validate a conceptual point. Correspondingly, the selection of country cases is based on their representative character for the conceptual argument at hand. Our empirical vignettes draw primarily on paired comparisons of "most similar" countries: Brazil and Indonesia, Turkey and South Africa, as well as Thailand and Vietnam. These pairs are structured similarly: They follow the same overall growth model but differ in their institutional and political approaches toward addressing the resulting structural vulnerabilities. While three of these countries were able to uphold growth overall in the time period under scrutiny (Indonesia, Turkey, and Vietnam), the other three experienced a substantial decline in their growth rates and stagnation or outright economic crisis (Brazil, South Africa, and Thailand; see Table 3). A notable finding in Section 5 relates to our argument that growth models depend on certain political-institutional constellations. We show that the less vulnerable economies in our sample, Indonesia, Turkey, and Vietnam, have associations or similar (informal) institutional arrangements that are a crucial element in the accommodation between various social groups, as well as between the state and business. These play little or no role in the more vulnerable cases of Brazil, South Africa, and Thailand. This shows that, at least within the limited time period studied in this Element, the political stabilization of a growth model rests on broad societal support and functional mechanisms for state-business relations.

3 A Typology of Peripheral Growth Models

In this section, we first introduce different types of peripheral growth models that will guide the study of growth trajectories of selected emerging capitalist economies in the following sections. We then analyze several descriptive statistics in order to identify growth models in our sample countries over the past two decades.

3.1 Adapting Growth Model Typologies to Emerging Capitalist Economies

Being aware of the fallacies of typological theorizing (Hay, 2020), we acknowledge the limits of this framework right from the start. As ideal types are "*limiting* concept[s] with which the real situation or action is *compared*" (Weber, 1947 [1922], 93, original emphasis), our typology is primarily meant to be a heuristic device for comparative analysis (Swedberg, 2018, 189–90). It aims to reduce the complexity of contemporary capitalist development in emerging economies and to provide the conceptual basis for hypothesis formulation and empirical research. Of course, it does not claim to cover all growth experiences in the global South. Nor should the aim be to group all countries into ideal-typical categories. In reality, many cases display features of several of the ideal types mentioned below, thereby creating tensions with the temporal and spatial specificity of growth trajectories. Needless to say, not every country exhibits a well-defined growth model at any point in time, as there is ample evidence of crisis and stagnation in peripheral economies.

The identification of growth models starts with a basic distinction between their main components of aggregate demand: private consumption, government consumption, investment, and (net) exports. Next to these broad types of growth models, we introduce several subtypes, which, on the one hand, capture the main sources of growth experiences of emerging economies identified in the literature and, on the other hand, differ with regard to their degree of economic vulnerability (Table 2).

Table 2 Growth models in emerging capitalist economies

Type	Export-led		Consumption-led		Investment-led	
Subtype	Manufacturing-based	Commodities-based	Wage-based	Debt-based	Domestically-based	FDI-based
Growth driver	Price and non-price competitiveness	Commodity prices	Real wage growth	Portfolio inflows	Fiscal policy and domestic drivers	FDI inflows
Vulnerability	Lower	Higher	Lower	Higher	Lower	Higher

Source: Own elaboration.

Due to their less developed productive structure and lower capital stock, investments play a much more important role in emerging economies than in advanced economies. The recent experience of India or China exemplifies this point (Ahuja & Nabar, 2012; ten Brink, 2019).[7] Therefore, we propose a third type of growth model – investment-led growth – which has so far not been identified in the core countries (see, e.g., Picot, 2021; Baccaro & Hadziabdic, 2024). Moreover, due to their position in the world economy, emerging economies are generally characterized by higher vulnerability – even though their vulnerability may vary with their economic profile and regime type. This elevates the possible negative impacts of variables linked to their international interdependencies (Bonizzi et al., 2020), such as massive capital outflows as witnessed during the 2008 global financial crisis and the beginning of the COVID-19 pandemic. In order to account for this salient feature of growth in peripheral economies, we introduce the separate dimension of vulnerability, ranging from low to high, depending on the respective growth driver. The latter are factors, which are "not themselves part of aggregate income but influence the growth of its components" (Kohler & Stockhammer, 2022, 1319).

Against this backdrop, we distinguish the following peripheral growth model types and their respective subtypes:

(i) **Export-led growth models:** These growth models are defined as sustained periods of growth that are primarily driven by exports. Here, it matters substantially which sectors of the economy are the main exporters. Economic complexity, value added, and the structure of global markets vary widely and have important repercussions on growth trajectories. Arguably, the main export sectors in emerging economies are either manufacturing or commodities. Services such as tourism are a third "export" sector that accounts for a sizable share of GDP growth, albeit mainly for smaller developing countries such as Bhutan and Jamaica.

  (1) *Manufacturing-based export-led growth* refers to episodes when the main export sectors are in manufacturing. Countries can thrive based on higher price or non-price competitiveness, depending on the degree of price elasticity of demand of different manufacturing sectors and the structure of global markets. But typically, with poor technological capabilities, prices have a binding constraint on the manufacturing-based growth models of most low- and middle-income countries. Consequently, there is a tendency to repress real

---

[7] This is not to say, of course, that there is no potential for – or even dire need of – investment in many of the advanced economies as well. However, due to much lower capital stocks, this need is arguably much more pronounced in emerging economies.

wage growth and, as a result, domestic consumption in economies with a large export sector is generally lower. This has negative repercussions on domestic welfare and inequality in the short term. However, in a mid- to long-term perspective, a manufacturing-based export-led growth model potentially leads to more sustainable and inclusive development, especially if a country manages to transition from price to non-price competitiveness (product differentiation, quality, and innovation), as exemplified by Korea.[8]

(2) *Commodities-based export-led growth* refers to episodes when the main export sectors are natural goods. This holds true for the vast majority of peripheral economies. Lacking short-term alternative options, many countries, by necessity, adopt such a development strategy. However, this type of growth model has potentially destabilizing effects. First, commodity prices are highly volatile and often lead to pronounced boom-bust scenarios. Second, rising commodity prices generally trigger capital inflows from abroad, resulting in a loss of competitiveness for manufacturing and thereby gradually leading to deindustrialization (the Dutch Disease phenomenon). Further negative effects relate to political instability and armed conflicts arising from distributional conflicts over the exploitation of commodity rents (the so-called resource curse).

(ii) **Consumption-led growth models**: These growth models are defined as sustained periods of growth primarily driven by private consumption. Household consumption can be financed by two main sources: wages or debt. Hence, we further distinguish between two main subtypes here, wage-based growth and debt-based growth.

(1) *Wage-based consumption-led growth* refers to episodes when sustained real wage growth leads to higher incomes, which in turn fuel household consumption expenditure. Increased demand may then spur further investment by companies, resulting in a virtuous cycle of capital accumulation. Politically, such a growth model can be induced by several policies, such as minimum wage increases, public sector pay increases, or the strengthening of collective bargaining institutions and trade unions. We witnessed such a growth model in many countries in the two decades after World War II. However, the model has an inherent tendency to fuel inflation through continuous wage pushes and to squeeze the profits of capital (Baccaro et al., 2022, 506).

---

[8] Still, we need to add the caveat that the current geopolitical dynamics pose further challenges to this type of growth model in light of increasing trade frictions and protectionism.

(2) *Debt-based consumption-led growth* refers to episodes when credit expansion leads to higher disposable incomes of households, fueling consumption expenditure. This is particularly relevant for capital goods industries and real estate. One of the main drivers of debt-based models is capital inflows from abroad, which can drive down long-term interest rates and push up local asset prices. This may contribute to a credit boom, spurring domestic economic activity. However, relying too heavily on the inflow of foreign capital in turn creates vulnerability, as the danger of sudden stops and boom-bust cycles looms large.[9]

(iii) ***Investment-led growth models:*** These growth models are defined by sustained periods of growth that are primarily driven by investment. Investment is based on two main sources: domestic or foreign capital.

(1) *Domestically-based investment-led growth* refers to episodes when increased investments in infrastructure, housing, plants, or machinery fuel growth. Fiscal policy is arguably one of the main drivers of such a growth model, albeit there are numerous other possible drivers of (private) investment (such as new technologies, for instance). Beyond boosting demand in the short run, investments build long-term economic capacity, enhance productivity, and create additional employment. If investment predominately takes place in (residential) housing, there may be overlaps with the debt-based growth model discussed earlier. Instability in this model may result mainly from overproduction and overindebtedness of the business sector.[10]

(2) *FDI-based investment-led growth* refers to episodes when investments by multinational corporations (MNCs) in local production plants drive the growth model. This model, by definition, heavily relies on a continuous inflow of FDI. Interrupting these flows, for example, through the relocation of production plants by MNCs, represents the

---

[9] Of course, the debt-led model might also be fueled by remittances inflows, which tend to be more stable and even countercyclical. However, remittances are significantly more important for smaller less developed countries such as Lebanon or Kosovo (Wanklin, 2025).

[10] The issue of "overproduction" or "overinvestments" have different interpretations, with potentially different solutions. From a PKE perspective (despite meaningful internal debates, such as between Kaleckians and Sraffians), it is important to remember that investments are also a source of demand – the expenditure on capital goods – which via the multiplier further generates income for households (via wages) and therefore more demand for the whole economy. Moreover, it also boosts demand within the capital goods sector itself (the production of machines by other machines). Over time, however, there must be enough effective demand in the economy to keep investments going. If the final effective demand falls, at some point utilization rates may decline and/or profitability fall, which then leads to an investment slowdown. To the extent investments are financed in the banking/financial system, there is also a risk of growing private indebtedness.

main source of vulnerability for this type of growth model. In a mid-term perspective, this translates into a structural challenge for an FDI-led development strategy, as MNCs often are not willing to share advanced technology with host countries (Gertler, 2003; Liu, 2008). Consequently, the latter eventually might be stuck in a so-called middle-income trap, which refers to a loss of competitiveness in labor-intensive manufacturing, while still not having reached the capacities for advanced production and R&D related activities.

We restrict ourselves to these types of growth models, which cover the main options for pursuing growth in emerging economies. Other models, which are, for example, based on remittances, foreign aid, or tourism, are mainly relevant for smaller developing countries with specific economic endowments and are hardly comparable to other economies.

3.2 Identifying Peripheral Growth Models

To develop an empirical approximation to growth models in ECEs, we use the relative contributions of aggregate demand components to GDP growth. Following Hein et al. (2021), we calculate the relative contributions to GDP growth by dividing the change in one aggregate demand component (e.g., C for private consumption) by the change in GDP (Y: dC/dY). We are aware of the limitations of this method, which is less suited to specify the role of exports, the vulnerability of growth models, and their main drivers (Kohler & Stockhammer, 2022, 1318–19; Baccaro & Hadziabdic, 2024, 1330–31). Traditionally relying on net exports as one component of aggregate demand, this method tends to either over- or underemphasize the actual role of exports for a country's growth model. Many emerging economies have a less sophisticated productive structure and thus have high volumes of consumption or capital goods imports. In addition, their major export items are commodities, that is, raw materials and agricultural goods. Due to the high share of imports that are consumed by the private and/or the public sector of these economies, their massive gross exports often do not show up in growth contributions, where net exports are generally low or even negative. Therefore, we focus on gross instead of net exports.[11] In

---

[11] An alternative option would be to use input-output tables and calculate the imports-adjusted demand components, distinguishing between the volumes of imports that are absorbed by each demand component (Baccaro & Hadziabdic, 2024, 1331). Input-output tables are provided, for instance, by the OECD for sixty-six countries, which is the largest coverage available. However, it does not cover all the countries in our sample. Consequently, we use the traditional growth decomposition approach, relying on national accounts data provided by the United Nations (2025).

order to identify the vulnerabilities and drivers of each growth model, we employ qualitative case vignettes in the subsequent sections of this Element.

The period of observation depends on the availability of harmonized data (mostly 2000–2022), which we further split into two subperiods (2001–2011 and 2012–2022). The rationale for this division relates to the main growth drivers of peripheral growth models: the years 2011 and 2012 mark the end of the commodity super cycle, a peak of capital flows to ECEs, and a plateauing of FDI inflows to ECEs (Miranda-Agrippino & Rey, 2022; Jungmann, 2023; see Section 4). Furthermore, prior studies have identified growth model shifts in several ECEs around the year 2011 as well (Campana et al., 2024).

Table 3 displays the results for the fourteen selected ECEs. While ECE annual growth rates are, on average, much higher than in the United States or European countries in that period (2.15 percent for the US and 1.56 percent for the EU respectively, see World Bank, 2025), data for some ECEs, notably Argentina, Brazil, Russia, and South Africa, also show a steep decline from the 2000s to the 2010s. These countries seem to follow those vulnerable trajectories of boom-bust growth as laid out earlier. Thailand is another case that experiences a substantial drop in its GDP growth between the two periods, although less pronounced than the other four countries. The rest of the countries in our sample, notably China, Indonesia, and Vietnam, also show relatively declining growth rates overall, but appear to have been more successful in sustaining growth. Egypt and Turkey are the only countries in the sample whose growth rates increase in the later period.

According to this data, there is not one single growth model for ECEs (Table 3). In general, however, private consumption plays an important role in many countries in our sample. Only China and Nigeria exhibit a slightly lower but still significant contribution of private consumption to GDP growth. South Africa appears to align with the consumption-led model, although government consumption plays an important role as well. The same holds true for Turkey, albeit with less pronounced government consumption. As we will demonstrate in the next section, household indebtedness has been driving this trend in both economies. While credit expansion in South Africa was especially salient in the period before the global financial crisis, it became more important in the subsequent period in Turkey. In both cases, capital inflows have been drivers of debt-based growth (Section 4). Wage-based growth models have been rare since the 1980s – with Israel between 2008 and 2018 as an exception (Bondy & Maggor, 2024). Consequently, we do not find it in our sample.

Overall, government consumption is less significant than the other demand components in our sample countries (Figure 3). Only Argentina, and to some extent Mexico and Nigeria, exhibit a relatively high degree of this component.

Table 3 Relative contributions to GDP growth in emerging capitalist economies, 2001–2022

	GDP Annual growth		Private consumption		Government consumption		Investment		Exports	
	2001–11	2012–22	2001–11	2012–22	2001–11	2012–22	2001–11	2012–22	2001–11	2012–22
Argentina	5,00%	0,50%	0,64	0,46	0,13	0,51	0,27	0,26	0,14	−0,03
Brazil	3,87%	0,68%	0,65	1,01	0,18	0,05	0,25	−0,55	0,18	0,45
China	10,90%	6,20%	0,33	0,39	0,14	0,16	0,50	0,40	0,28	0,16
Egypt	4,74%	4,77%	0,76	0,85	0,10	0,06	0,17	0,13	0,26	0,14
India	7,10%	5,98%	0,49	0,61	0,10	0,09	0,57	0,26	0,40	0,17
Indonesia	5,23%	3,99%	0,50	0,57	0,14	0,06	0,36	0,28	0,33	0,21
Mexico	7,50%	2,73%	0,70	1,10	0,34	−0,06	0,07	0,11	0,22	0,01
Nigeria	4,40%	2,64%	0,39	0,35	0,17	0,29	0,27	0,32	0,86	0,45
Russia	4,73%	1,05%	0,79	0,40	0,08	0,15	0,37	−0,32	0,33	0,18
South Africa	3,36%	0,88%	0,75	0,96	0,21	0,24	0,38	−0,17	0,17	0,39
Thailand	4,51%	1,91%	0,46	0,67	0,19	0,16	0,32	0,19	1,00	0,25
Turkey	5,72%	6,28%	0,63	0,62	0,13	0,11	0,51	0,16	0,27	0,22
Vietnam	9,77%	6,37%	0,51	0,51	0,13	0,07	0,39	0,37	0,56	1,38

Note: We have calculated the compound annual growth rate (CAGR) for each aggregate demand component for each period. CAGR represents the annual growth rate required to move from the starting GDP to the final GDP over a specified period, assuming constant growth at this rate. By smoothing out yearly fluctuations, it eliminates the effects of volatility and is well-suited for long-term comparisons and trend analysis. For private consumption, we use household consumption expenditure; for investments, we use gross capital formation; for government consumption, we use general government final consumption expenditure; for net exports, we calculate separately the growth rates of exports and imports of goods and services. The absolute contribution for each aggregate demand component was obtained by multiplying their CAGR by their average weight shares in each period. Finally, we normalized them to obtain their relative contributions. The sum of private and government consumption, investment, and net exports equals to one. As the table displays exports rather than net exports, the sum will typically exceed unity.

Source: United Nations National Accounts, constant 2015 prices, GDP expenditure approach, extracted on January 12, 2025; own calculations.

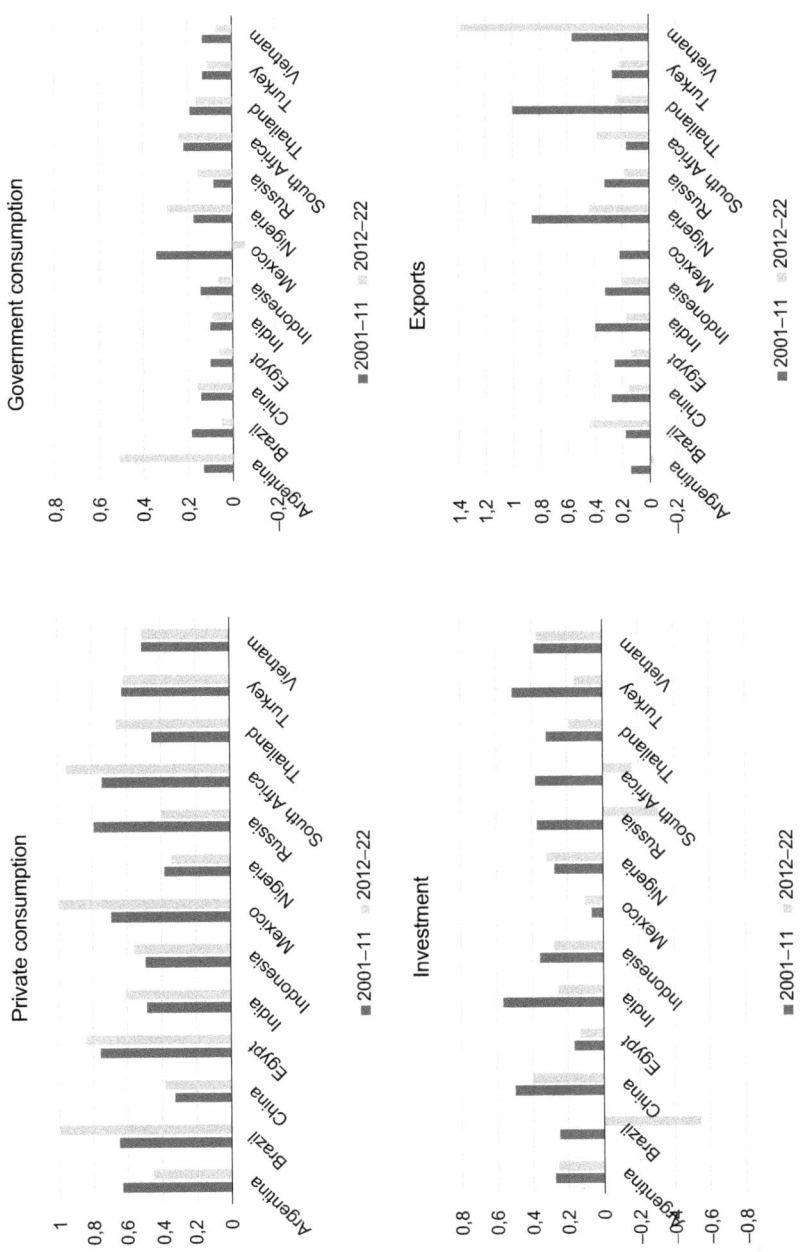

Figure 3 Relative contributions to growth by demand component, 2001–2022

Source: see Table 3.

In the former, this is mainly due to a sustained period of expansionary fiscal and social policies under the Kirchner governments (2003–2015) (Ianni, 2024), with public administration as well as educational and health services being major drivers of GDP growth (Baccaro & Hadziabdic, 2025).

Investment, by contrast, seems to play a major role in many countries in our sample. Notably, China and India display a strong investment-led profile similar to that of Turkey and South Africa, though this tendency is declining sharply in the latter two cases. In all the cases, the construction sector plays an important role, contributing up to 34 percent to overall GDP growth in China in the 2010s, for instance (Baccaro & Hadziabdic, 2025). Thailand and Vietnam also feature a significant share of investment in their GDP growth, but mainly in the manufacturing sector, dominated by foreign MNCs. However, this share is declining substantially in Thailand, while Vietnam seems to uphold it in the period 2012–2022 as well. As we will show in the next section, investment in both countries is heavily driven by FDI (Section 4).

Finally, exports are very volatile but still significant in countries such as Brazil, Indonesia, Nigeria, Thailand, and Vietnam. While Thailand and Vietnam are highly integrated into global production networks, there is no country in the sample that displays a proper manufacturing-based export-led growth model, relying on indigenous manufacturing capacities. Given their heavy GVC participation, both Thailand and Vietnam only feature very high gross exports, while their net export contributions to growth are negligible or even negative. There is a striking similarity to the FDI-led models of East Central Europe, which also exhibit high volumes of gross exports, while foreign investment is the main driver of GDP growth (Avlijaš et al., 2021; Bohle & Regan, 2021). Brazil and Indonesia, by contrast, are part of a larger group of peripheral economies featuring commodities-based export-led growth, where commodity revenues at least temporarily serve as a basis for redistributive policies supporting domestic consumption (Nölke et al., 2020, 137–9, Passos & Morlin, 2022; Schedelik et al., 2023). As we demonstrate in the subsequent section, both countries managed the vulnerabilities associated with this type of growth model very differently.

In sum, investment and private consumption are the key contributors to growth in the countries in our sample, while government consumption and exports are less significant overall. This questions the popular diagnosis of emerging economy growth as being mainly export-led, as discussed in the experience of East Asian "tiger states" in the 1980s (World Bank, 1993) or the rise of the BRICS countries, especially China, in the 2000s (Feenstra & Wei, 2010). Further juxtaposing peripheral growth models with the consumption- and export-led models in advanced capitalist economies, we find investments to be heavily important for some ECEs, supporting our intuition for the addition of an investment-led growth model to the typology of an extended GM perspective. For a theory of capitalist diversity this should not be a surprising point to make since investments should be at the core of any theory about growth – and in fact has been for political economy scholarship of the so-called "golden age of capitalism" (Marglin & Schor, 1991; Schwartz & Tranøy, 2019) and earlier development theories, such as those associated with the model of import-substitution industrialization in the global South (Irwin, 2021). It stands that only investments, besides representing an increase in aggregate demand, also expand productive capacity. Consumption and export growth boost demand and thus the utilization of the capital stock, yet only investments increase the capital stock. This point is particularly salient for ECEs since they usually have a lower capital stock than advanced economies and need to invest in order to catch up. At the same time, since higher investments yield additional capacity, there is also a need to find demand for this increased productive capacity.

Systematically introducing the possibility of an investment-led growth model helps us to understand the various political-economic trajectories of high-growth economies. We can also learn from studies on former transition economies in Central and Eastern Europe, as well as Ireland, which pointed to an FDI-based model (e.g., Bohle & Regan, 2021). For instance, the macro-political and institutional factors that shore up and constantly challenge such an investment-led growth model vary with the latter's integration into the world economy and the type of investments within that model. For this reason, we later turn to a more qualitative vignette approach that is able to carve out potential causal effects supporting and sustaining an investment-led growth model by studying the growth trajectories of Thailand and Vietnam.

After all, and it is worth repeating, none of these models is dominant for ECEs as a group, and all types require differentiation. Table 4 proposes such a differentiation with a view toward exemplary cases. However, in contrast to the clear-cut growth models which could be found in Europe (only) before the global financial crisis (Baccaro & Pontusson, 2016; Hein et al., 2021), we should be careful with the neat categorization of countries into singular types. We find a much higher degree of hybridity for the growth models in ECEs. Moreover, traditional growth model decomposition may lead to misleading impressions, given the high export shares for FDI-based models and the (partial) utilization of commodity export revenues for the stimulation of domestic consumption in commodity-led models discussed earlier. Correspondingly, our simplified classification should be taken as an invitation for further research on how to understand the nature of peripheral growth models.

Table 4 Types of growth models and country cases

Type	Export-led		Consumption-led		Investment-led	
Subtype	Manufacturing-based	Commodities-based	Wage-based	Debt-based	Domestically-based	FDI-based
Country cases	**	Indonesia, Brazil	**	Turkey, South Africa	China	Vietnam, Thailand

Note: ** Not found in our sample.
Source: Own elaboration.

Moreover, we posit that the considerable heterogeneity within the category of ECEs demands an institutionally sensitive process when classifying growth models. In order to substantiate this claim, we move to the level of international interdependencies of peripheral growth models (Section 4) and their political underpinnings (Section 5). Through the study of commodities-based export-led growth (Brazil and Indonesia), debt-based consumption-led growth (South Africa and Turkey), and FDI-based investment-led growth (Thailand and Vietnam), we show how the international insertion of a country's growth model shapes its vulnerabilities toward exogenous shocks. Still, each paired comparison demonstrates that despite structural dependencies, governments in ECEs can successfully mitigate the vulnerabilities arising from similar peripheral growth models. This capacity does not only rest on appropriate macroeconomic policies, but also on certain macro-political conditions. Subsequently, we illustrate the importance of these various factors, which represent constellations neglected in the study of growth models in the global North.

4 International Interdependencies and Peripheral Growth Models

In the following, we analyze three peripheral growth models in more detail. By drawing on paired comparisons of "most similar" countries, we outline some core features of commodities-based, debt-based, and FDI-based growth models, their respective growth drivers, and short- or mid-term vulnerabilities (Table 5). Specific attention is given to the ability of national governments to manage these vulnerabilities, under specific political conditions, contrasting the idea that their economic models are essentially determined by global dependencies (e.g., Kvangraven et al., 2021; Alami et al., 2023). The GM perspective, with its emphasis on (short-term) economic policies, lends itself toward an identification of economic agency. In doing so, we are arguing that heterodox economic policies overall are more successful than the liberal orthodoxy in managing the vulnerabilities stemming from their insertion into the global economy during this particular time period (Alami & Dixon, 2020; Petry et al., 2024; Petry & Nölke, 2025). Correspondingly, we are looking at two types of causalities here. On the one hand, we are pointing out how external growth drivers (commodity prices, portfolio, and FDI flows) are co-constituting the three types of peripheral growth models. On the other hand, we are sketching how, in each of these types, macroeconomic and industrial policies can make a difference with regard to the degree of each vulnerability.

Table 5 Selected peripheral growth models and their vulnerabilities

Growth model	Commodity-based export-led	Debt-based consumption-led	FDI-based investment-led
Growth driver	Commodity prices	Portfolio inflows	FDI inflows
Vulnerability	Dutch disease, deindustrialization	Sudden stops, financial and currency crisis	MNC relocation, middle-income trap

Source: Own elaboration.

4.1 Commodity Price Cycles and Export-Led Growth Models

Recently, GM scholarship has begun to study export-led growth models, especially the commodity-based subtype. Arguably, this is one of the most prevalent peripheral growth models globally (Schedelik et al., 2023). This model heavily relies on the development of commodity prices, which are set on global markets with little or no pricing power for producer countries. In addition, commodity prices are characterized by large swings, dubbed commodity super cycles, where prices rise sharply for several years before plummeting (Erten & Ocampo, 2013). Commodity price fluctuations overproportionally affect developing and emerging economies, which, on average, are less diversified and more commodity-dependent than advanced economies. These price cycles not only have a direct impact on export volumes and earnings, but also on macroeconomic stability, as economic activity in commodity-dependent ECEs closely mirrors the price movements of their major export items (IMF, 2012, 125). Here, we can draw on decades of development studies research, which has pointed toward the significant macroeconomic effects of an overreliance on natural resource extraction (see the literature on the "resource curse," cf. Ross, 2015).

The most important mechanism associated with fluctuations in commodity prices is the so-called "Dutch Disease" – termed after the economic side-effects of natural gas discoveries in the Netherlands in the 1950s (Corden, 1984). It refers to the real appreciation of the currency due to huge capital inflows into investment projects in the booming commodity sectors and/or large increases in commodity revenues during boom periods (Frankel, 2010, 20). This results in increased domestic income and spending by the private and especially public sector, leading to higher prices and output in the nontradables sectors and consequently to higher wages across the economy (the so-called "spending effect"). At the same time, capital and labor move from other parts of the economy to the booming commodity sectors, which results in rising prices of nontradables vis-à-vis other tradables (the so-called "resource movement effect"). Both effects lead to a real exchange rate appreciation and, therefore, to a loss of international competitiveness and declining output in the manufacturing sectors and, hence, to deindustrialization (Brahmbhatt et al., 2010). The predicament of the "Dutch Disease" is much less likely to occur in advanced economies that have developed a strong reliance on exports (such as Germany). These economies never fully tilt toward structural dependency – not least because the market structures for manufactured goods and commodities are fundamentally different: "what you export matters" (Hausmann et al., 2007). More specifically, avenues for diversification and technological upgrading are limited for most commodity-dependent developing and emerging economies, and depend on sustained political efforts, which are negatively affected by commodity price swings (UNCTAD, 2021).

The reliance on commodity exports is a recurring and prevalent feature of most developing and emerging economies. In the 2018–2019 period, 101 countries out of 195 UNCTAD member states, that is, 53 percent, were commodity-dependent, that is, with a commodity export product share of more than 60 percent (UNCTAD, 2021, 5). Beyond that, we can identify a correlation between the degree of commodity dependence, that is, commodity exports as a share of merchandise exports, and the contribution of commodity exports to a country's gross domestic product (Figure 4). A higher share of commodity export dependence is associated with a higher share of commodity exports in a country's GDP. Commodity dependence, thereby can be as high as 99.8 percent in the case of Iraq and even 100 percent in the case of South Sudan. Furthermore, several countries rely on only one or a few commodities. Countries such as Iraq (93.5 percent), Angola (88 percent), Chad (79.6 percent), and Guinea-Bissau (88.4 percent) depend heavily on the export of one single product (UNCTAD, 2019).

In the recent past, China's rapid industrialization and the related output growth in the 2000s generated immense demand for primary products. From 1997 to 2017, China's share of global energy consumption more than doubled, from 11 to 23 percent, while its share of global metals consumption even increased fivefold, from 10 to 50 percent (World Bank, 2018, 11). In comparison, advanced economies' share of global energy and metals consumption declined from 50 to 40 percent and 70 to 30 percent, respectively, in the same period. This demand shock fueled a sustained commodity price boom, which lasted until the early 2010s. The commodity super cycle came to a halt during

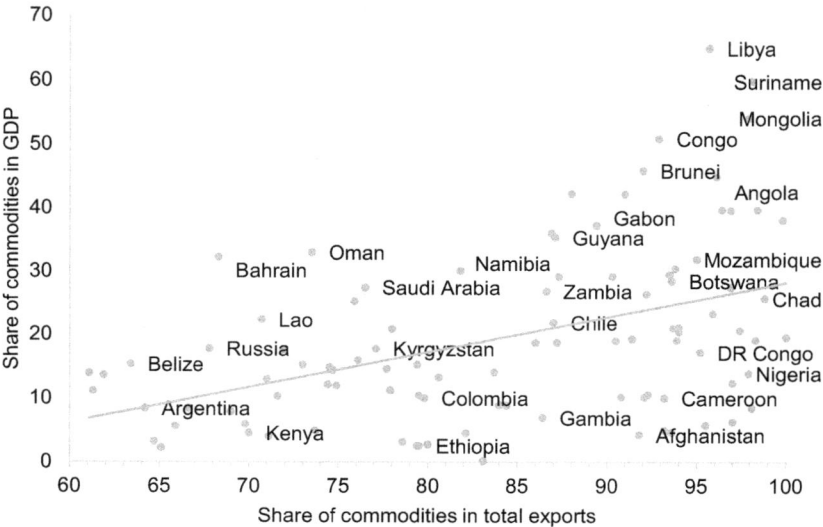

Figure 4 Commodity dependence of developing and emerging economies
Source: Own elaboration based on UNCTAD 2021

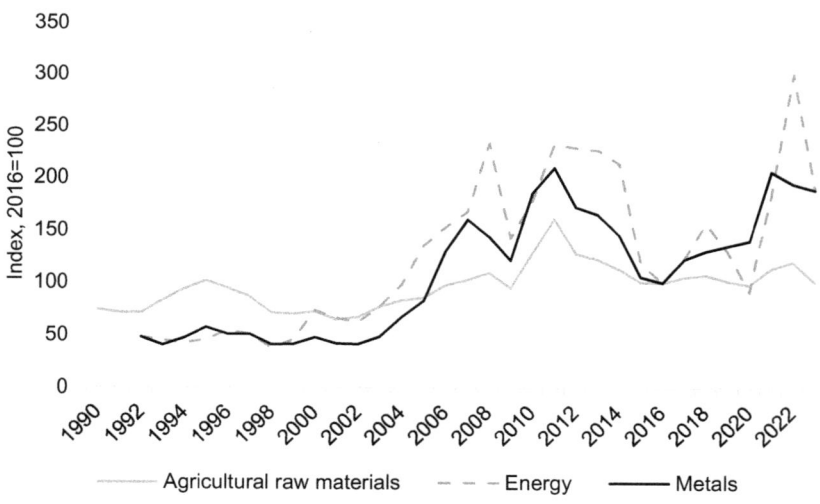

Figure 5 Commodity price cycles
Source: Own elaboration based on IMF, Primary Commodity Price System

the GFC and particularly after 2011, when commodity prices contracted sharply (see Figure 5).

We can see the effects of these fluctuations on growth models by comparing Brazil and Indonesia, which are both commodity exporters and of a similar size.

In both countries, the change in the growth trajectory at the end of the 2000s is striking, also in comparison with other major emerging economies (Section 3). Whereas exports were growth drivers for the two countries in the early 2000s, they were both hit hard by the strong reduction in export revenues after the end of the commodity boom that had been driven by China. In other words, the investment-led growth model in China created the demand for resources provided by extractivist suppliers with their commodities-based export-led growth model, only to increase pressure for adjustment when prices fell.

The growth models of the two economies, however, reacted differently to the end of the commodity cycle. Growth in Brazil collapsed, whereas it remained stable in Indonesia (Table 3). While Indonesia was able to retain a high contribution of investments alongside private consumption when exports dwindled, Brazil was unable to stimulate along similar lines. Furthermore, private consumption – together with government consumption – had to carry the whole burden of growth stimulation in Brazil in the medium-term, in line with the notion of a wage-based recovery but increasingly also rising consumer debt. In other words, while Brazil shortly moved from a commodity-based export-led model to a consumption-led model, Indonesia came to a more sustainable model based on investments and private consumption. Whereas Indonesia in this way managed to rebalance its growth model and diversify its export profile away from raw materials, Brazil's heavy reliance on commodity exports even intensified and peaked at almost 60 percent of total exports in 2021 (Figure 6).

Openness toward the global economy and pressures from financial subordination seem to be core factors here. Brazil is much more open toward foreign finance and trade, whereas Indonesia has followed a more protectionist path since the global financial crisis. Beginning during the second term of President Susilo Bambang Yudhoyono (2009–2014), Indonesia turned away from its previously rather orthodox neoliberal model (Jepson, 2020). In this case, protectionism refers both to financial flows – a legacy of the ill-fated opening of the financial sector after the 1998 Asian financial crisis (Pepinsky, 2013) – and trade, where the risk of deindustrialization via open borders for Chinese imports has been taken much more seriously than in Brazil. This means, in turn, that Brazil was not able to minimize its structural dependency on foreign demand and finance in the same way as Indonesia.

The governments led by the Brazilian Workers' Party (PT) embarked on a program for stimulating domestic demand via private consumption when the PT took power in 2003. Measures to alleviate poverty, raising the minimum wage, and the promotion of credit access for private households (partly through

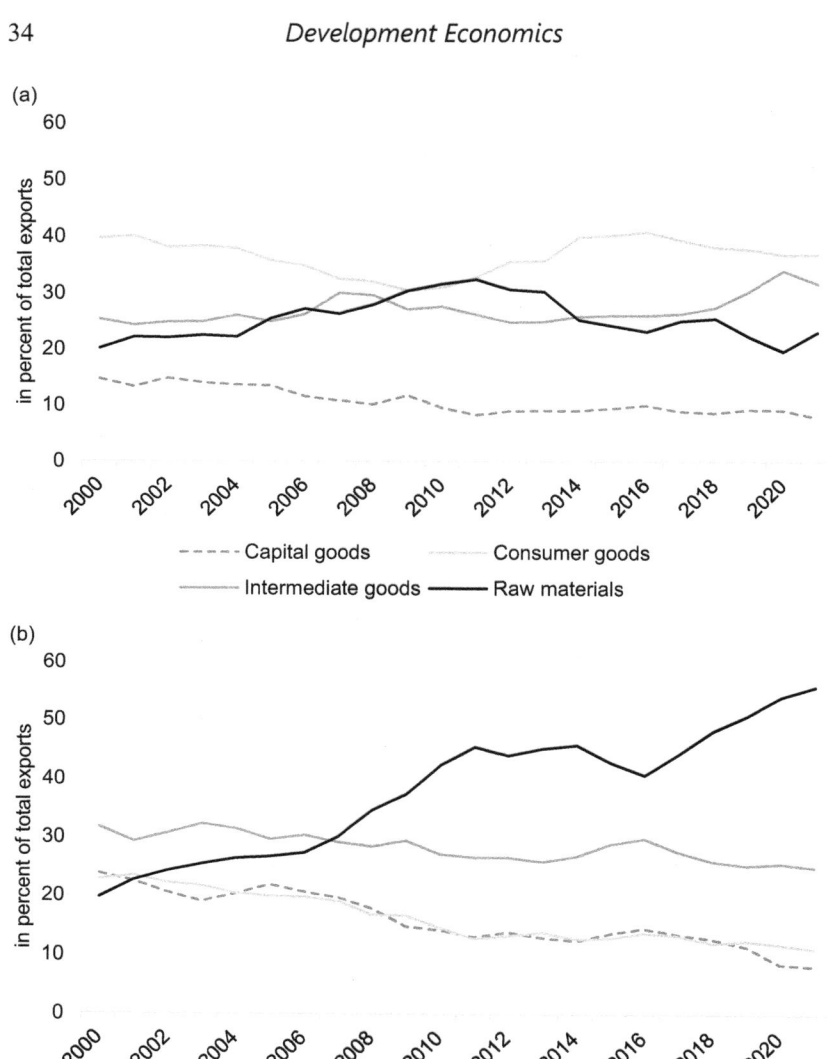

Figure 6 Export product share by stage of processing of Indonesia (a) and Brazil (b)

Source: Own elaboration based on WTO, World Integrated Trade Solution database

social transfers) were successful in stimulating domestic demand and reducing inequality (Passos & Morlin, 2022; Schedelik, 2023, 64–70). Yet, a large part of this additional demand was met by foreign companies, most notably from China. Furthermore, massive capital inflows led to a substantial overvaluation of the Real, proving a juggernaut for the domestic manufacturing sector and contributing to a sustained process of deindustrialization (Schedelik, 2023, 70–80). When the Brazilian economy recovered briefly after the GFC due to massive public investments in infrastructure and the expansion of subsidized credit, financial inflows surged to record levels (Gallagher & Prates, 2016). In this context, Brazil temporarily implemented capital controls and interventions in the foreign exchange market, but powerful transnationally oriented financial capital prevented the introduction of really effective controls (Dierckx, 2015, 154–5).

The broader macroeconomic trends, mainly rising Chinese demand for commodities, affected investment flows, which mostly targeted the booming commodity sectors rather than manufacturing, counteracting several industrial policies of the time (Mesquita Moreira et al., 2020, 2). These industrial policies included huge tax exemptions for the domestic industry under the so-called "Greater Brazil Plan" launched in 2011, which led to a slowdown in budgetary revenue growth. Together with rising spending on pensions, social benefits, and an array of subsidies to uphold domestic consumption, this contributed to a rapidly deteriorating fiscal situation (Holland, 2019; Ricz & Schedelik, 2023). When tax revenues shrank with the end of the commodity super cycle (and it became clear that expectations about the oil rents to be extracted from new hydrocarbon discoveries were overconfident), further stimulation of private domestic demand became politically highly contested, and the consumption-led growth model turned sour (Nölke et al., 2022; Passos & Morlin, 2022).

Indonesia, in turn, has been more restrictive with regard to imports and financial flows, also as a reaction to previous destabilization: "Since the 1997–98 Asian financial crisis, Indonesian economic policy has consistently prioritized stability over riskier pathways to economic growth" (Rajah, 2018, 2). President Joko Widodo (2014–2024) further strengthened the move toward neo-developmentalism, which began during the second term of his predecessor, Susilo Bambang Yudhoyono (Warburton, 2016). Correspondingly, the government compensated for the end of the commodity boom with massive public investment, predominantly in construction and infrastructure projects, but also in "downstreaming," where raw materials are processed domestically rather than exported (Camba et al., 2022). For example, in the electric vehicles value chain, Indonesia sought to restrict the export of unprocessed mineral ores in order to encourage the localization of a domestic mineral beneficiation industry. This is a strategy that can be seen as a reaction to China's increasing imports of cheap mineral ores (such as nickel) to produce electric vehicle batteries (Schröder & Iwasaki, 2023). Similarly, the government has put into place a number of measures to limit imports, particularly of consumer goods. Together with expanding government social programs, the jobs created by these activities have contributed to the strong growth of domestic consumption (OECD, 2018a, 131–3). Similar observations can be made with regard to financial flows. Again, the Indonesian government has consciously put a premium on stability. Not only is the economy less integrated into GVCs than other countries in the region (OECD, 2018a, 133), but the Indonesian government also puts a strong emphasis on limited vulnerability with regard to global financial markets. This includes capping external borrowing as well as the current account deficit, combined with the accumulation of considerable foreign exchange reserves (Rajah, 2018, 3). The restrictive Indonesian strategy was supported by its political system with a high concentration of power in the presidency, whereas the more fragmented Brazilian system allowed for more influential lobbying by the financial sector (Nölke et al., 2020, 120–2).

To sum up, both Brazil and Indonesia followed export-led growth paths during the commodity boom period, partly driven by demand from China. When the super cycle came to an end, Indonesia was less pressured by capital outflows than Brazil, enabling its government to expand fiscally and stimulate investment and consumption to boost growth. Brazil, in contrast, had – also fiscally – bolstered the expansion of domestic markets and consumption, but with rising private indebtedness and strengthened political pressure from a coalition between financial capital, the traditional middle class, and increasingly from industrialists (Marques, 2025), ran into crisis and stagnation. By pursuing a more protectionist approach, Indonesia has been able to rebalance its growth model toward investment and consumption and diversify its export structure away from raw materials. Brazil, by contrast, has even deepened its heavy reliance on commodity exports in the recent past. Needless to say, smaller developing and emerging countries, that is the vast majority, are even more prone to the pitfalls of commodities-based growth. Still, the case of Indonesia demonstrates that mid-sized emerging economies are not necessarily helpless vis-à-vis global commodity price cycles.

4.2 Financial Cycles and Consumption-Led Growth Models

Further important international interdependencies for developing and emerging economies stem from their integration into the global financial system. It has been shown that the global financial crisis has been a watershed for the trajectory of growth models in advanced economies (Hein et al., 2021; Kohler & Stockhammer, 2022). Arguably, the GFC played a similar role in some ECEs, where it fostered a change of growth models (Akcay et al., 2022). More specifically, global financial markets shape political economies in the global South by means of subordinated financialization, potentially destabilizing domestic growth models via large-scale speculative financial flows and the dynamics of global financial cycles under US dollar hegemony (Bonizzi et al., 2022). Financial subordination thereby refers to many developing and emerging economies' strong reliance on external borrowing and the resulting vulnerability to sudden capital flows and exchange rate swings. Due to the still prominent role of foreign currency-denominated debt (famously called the "original sin," cf. Eichengreen & Hausmann, 2005) and foreign investors in local currency bond markets ("original sin redux," cf. Carstens & Shin, 2019), a large portion of these countries' debt induces currency mismatches in the event of exchange rate depreciation which increases the risk of local financial crises. Positive inflows can drive down long-term interest rates and push up local asset prices. This may assist domestic economic activity, contributing to a credit boom. Large negative portfolio flows, however, very often trigger financial crises with severe domestic macroeconomic consequences (Kohler, 2022).

Since the early 2000s, capital flows to developing and emerging economies have risen markedly, as international investors increasingly discovered "emerging market" assets as a promising investment (Figure 7). In particular, portfolio flows have recently reached unprecedented levels, outpacing FDI (Molina & Viani, 2019). A recent empirical literature, therefore, has investigated the drivers of these flows (see Koepke, 2019 for an overview). Global risk aversion

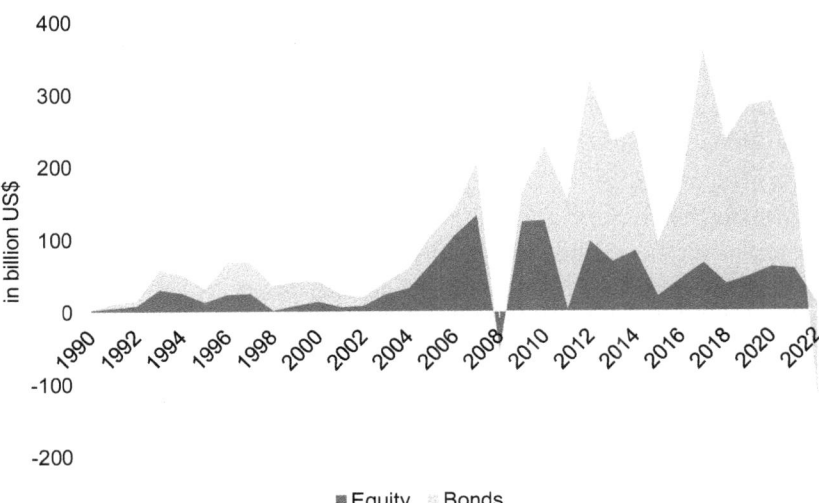

Figure 7 Portfolio capital inflows to developing and emerging economies
Source: Own elaboration based on IMF, Balance of Payments database; World Bank, International Debt Statistics

and a strong US dollar are negatively correlated with capital inflows to developing and emerging economies, whereas output growth in the recipient countries is positively correlated (Molina & Viani, 2019, 4). In addition, commodity prices are another important determinant of capital inflows for commodity-dependent countries, even since the nineteenth century (Reinhart et al., 2016). Although many ECEs have sought to protect their economies against financial volatilities by imposing capital controls and accumulating foreign reserves, they still tend to be affected significantly (Bauerle Danzmann et al., 2017). As capital flows toward developing and emerging economies are predominately pro-cyclical, they tend to exaggerate boom-bust cycles and seriously impinge on their domestic macroeconomic stability (Akyüz, 2022).

We can observe the impact of global capital cycles on peripheral growth models by comparing South Africa and Turkey, which are both relatively open toward international financial markets and of a similar size. Both countries experienced debt-based growth trajectories recently, culminating in major crises. Whereas Turkey's growth model can be classified as regular domestic demand-led before the global financial crisis, it shifted toward a debt-based model in the post-GFC period (Akcay et al., 2022). South Africa, by contrast, sustained a debt-based growth model throughout the 2000s and 2010s, despite a major recession induced by the GFC (Akcay et al., 2022). Both countries exhibit different types of debt booms, however. Whereas South Africa experienced a classical housing bubble, similar to countries such as Ireland or Spain in the European (semi-)periphery or the UK and the US before the GFC (Karwowski, 2018, 418), Turkey's growth model of the 2010s was based on a corporate debt bubble, which resulted in a classical currency-and-debt crisis (Akcay & Güngen, 2022). In both cases, large inflows of foreign capital played a crucial role in fueling the debt booms (Figure 8).

Both South Africa and Turkey have been in a similar situation with regard to the potentially devastating effects of global capital cycles. Still, Turkey has managed the vagaries of these cycles better than South Africa, not only with regard to the attraction of capital inflows, but also in terms of GDP growth (Ay et al., 2016; Figure 9). After the GFC in particular, Turkey's GDP growth far exceeds that of South Africa, which entered into a phase of economic stagnation, characterized by high levels of unemployment, low growth, and extreme inequality (Nölke et al., 2020, 145). Arguably, we can explain this divergence by the Turkish turn toward a stronger focus on industrial development (Kutlay, 2020, 692–8) and several "unconventional" economic and monetary policies after the crisis (Zayim, 2022).

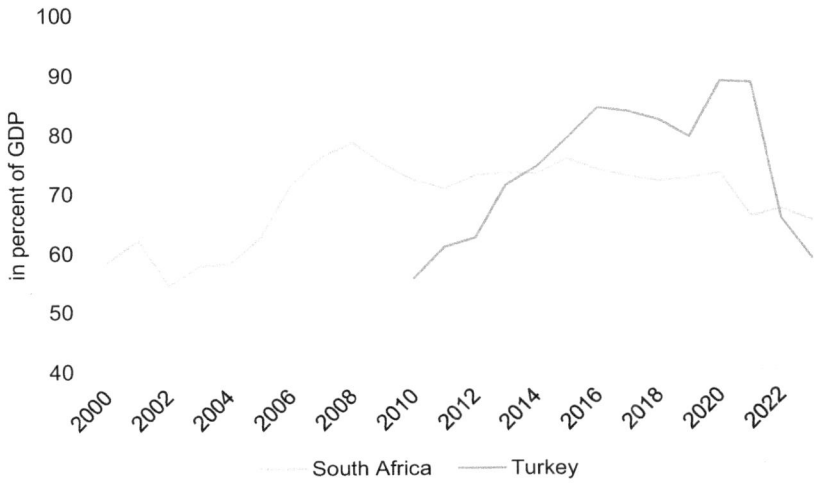

Figure 8 Private debt as a percentage of GDP in South Africa and Turkey
Source: Own elaboration based on IMF, Global Debt database

While some emerging economies reacted to the massive global liquidity during the quantitative easing (QE) phase in Europe and the United States with capital controls, with varying success (Section 4.1), the two debt-led countries analyzed here pursued different paths. South Africa, for its part, stuck largely to the neoliberal orthodoxy and even relaxed capital outflow restrictions in the wake of the crisis (Zayim, 2022, 544). Turkey, by contrast, implemented a series of unconventional policies such as re-regulating reserve requirements and adopting an asymmetric interest rate corridor (Apaydin & Çoban, 2023, 1056). Although the Turkish central bank modified the policy after the US Fed's taper tantrum in 2013, the Turkish economy navigated the turbulent post-GFC period better than many of its emerging market peers (Ay et al., 2016). As an example, the Turkish currency experienced far less volatility than other ECE currencies, and domestic credit growth was slowed (Kara, 2012, 18–9). Subsequently, the government implemented several industrial policies to shift the growth model toward more manufacturing exports, including neomercantilist policies for accessing new non-Western markets (Akcay & Jungmann, 2023, 547–9; Arnold & Naseemullah, 2024; Güngen & Akcay, 2024, 162–3). However, state interventionism had serious political consequences as well, consolidating President Erdoğan's increasingly authoritarian regime (Apaydin & Çoban, 2023; Güngen & Akcay, 2024, 163). Since 2018 at the latest, several regulatory agencies and the central bank became subject to political capture, forcing interest rates down to fuel credit expansion despite rising inflation (Çoban & Apaydin, 2025, 136–7).

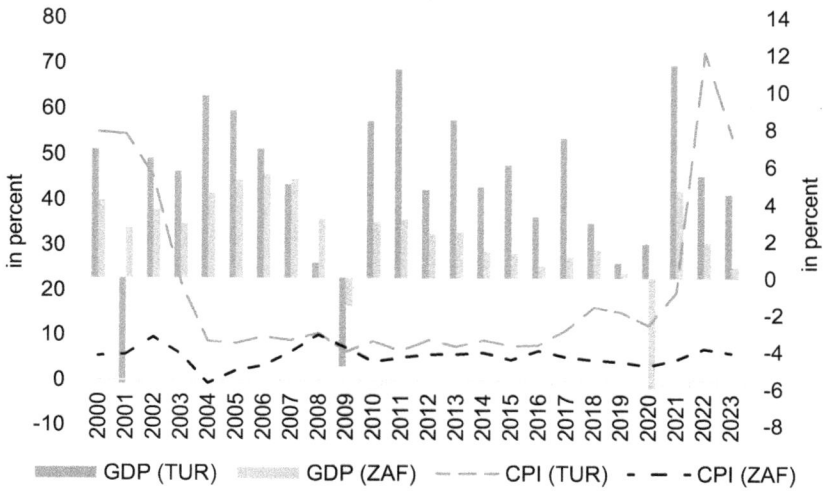

Figure 9 Annual growth of gross domestic product (right axis) and consumer price inflation (left axis) in Turkey and South Africa compared
Source: Own elaboration based on World Development Indicators

Consequently, the Turkish economy experienced a major currency crisis in 2018 and skyrocketing inflation of more than 70 percent in 2022 (Figure 9).

To sum up, both South Africa and Turkey pursued a debt-based growth model in the first two decades of the new millennium, in part driven by global excess liquidity before the GFC and during the QE episode. When the global financial cycle contracted during the GFC and the 2013 taper tantrum, Turkey managed the threat of massive capital outflows better than South Africa by adopting a set of unconventional monetary policies. This enabled its government to push for more industrial development and manufacturing exports. South Africa, by contrast, continuously relied on financialization and the debt-based model in spite of signs of stagnation and endemically low growth (Bonizzi & Karwowski, 2024, 309). By pursuing a more heterodox economic approach, Turkey has been able to rebalance its growth model somewhat toward manufacturing and exports. South Africa, following a strictly orthodox macroeconomic framework, has even deepened its heavy reliance on capital inflows until recently. Hence, the case of Turkey shows that emerging economies dispose of a set of economic policy measures to mitigate the vagaries of global financial cycles. However, Turkey's more recent political-economic trajectory warns of the serious medium to long-term negative side effects of certain debt-based growth models on the economy more generally and democratic institutions in particular. This has been amply demonstrated by economic history as well (Funke et al., 2016).

4.3 Foreign Direct Investment Flows and Investment-Led Growth Models

Growth model research on emerging economies has identified FDI-based growth models in several countries of the European periphery, such as Ireland and East Central Europe (Bohle & Regan, 2021; 2022; Ban & Adascalitei, 2022). In addition, earlier research in CPE has already shown how complete regions of the global economy, such as Central and Eastern Europe or Central America, have become structurally highly dependent on foreign investment (Nölke & Vliegenthart, 2009; Schneider, 2009). Since FDI comes from multinational firms, it does not merely reflect macroeconomic conditions, but also business strategies and global power relations (Strange, 1996). Hence, we need to take global corporations and their influence on national growth models seriously when studying the growth trajectories of developing and emerging countries (Kaczmarczyk, 2020; Bohle & Regan, 2021). Such an approach complements research on GVCs, which mainly operates at the sectoral level (Gereffi, 2018).

Foreign direct investment flows to developing and emerging economies have increased manifold since the 1990s, representing 70 percent of the world's total (Figure 10). This period has been marked by the information and communication technology revolution and the second phase of globalization, called the

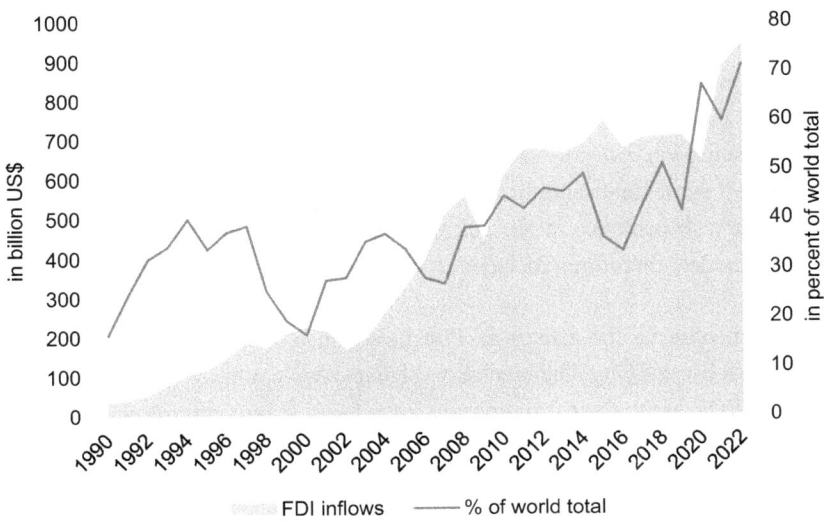

Figure 10 Foreign direct investment flows to developing and emerging economies

Source: Own elaboration based on UNCTAD FDI statistics

"second unbundling," as factories became separated internationally due to rapidly enhanced ways of communication and, hence, coordinating complex activities over long distances (Baldwin, 2016). Consequently, we have witnessed the rapid evolution of GVCs. More and more firms have organized production processes globally, offshoring parts or services to producers elsewhere. Therefore, GVC trade has increased significantly over time, accounting for about one-half of world trade recently (Antràs, 2020, 6). The rise of GVCs had important implications for developing and emerging economies, as it lowered the capabilities needed to enter such chains (Antràs, 2020, 11). However, not every type of GVC integration has proven equally supportive of sustainable growth and development. Commodity-based GVCs or lower value-added segments of production in general tend to exhibit lower economic returns for host countries. In addition, opportunities to upgrade from these lower production stages to higher-value-added stages, associated with more sophisticated technological know-how and more qualified employment, considerably depend on concerted industrial policies (Pipkin & Fuentes, 2017). Empirically, FDI and GVC integration are significantly correlated and mutually reinforce each other (Qiang et al., 2021, 6).

While FDI flows can lead to a transfer of technology toward developing and emerging economies, they also carry substantial disadvantages. Whereas the lead firms in global production chains are located in the high-income economies of the North, companies in the South often integrate in a subordinate position, being responsible for low-tech production, low-skills employment, and shouldering pollution-intensive activities (Wang et al., 2021). Furthermore, deep integration into GVCs negatively affects a country's national sovereignty with regard to labor or environmental regulation, as multinational corporations can sue host states via investor-state dispute settlement mechanisms in international investment agreements and threaten to disrupt GVC integration of the respective country (Moehlecke et al., 2023). The political choice for an FDI-based growth model, therefore, includes a certain "retreat of the state" (Strange, 1996).

We can observe the effects of FDI flows on growth models in emerging economies by studying Thailand and Vietnam, two countries with a very high share of FDI due to their proximity to East Asian manufacturing nations such as China, Korea, and Japan. So far, Southeast Asia is relatively underexplored in the GM literature. However, the region has been among the leading FDI destinations in the early 2020s, largely withstanding the global downward trend. In 2023 alone, the region received 226 billion US$ in FDI inflows with 1,568 greenfield announcements, a 42 percent increase from the previous year (UNCTAD, 2024, 7, 13–4). Comparing these countries to other FDI-dominated

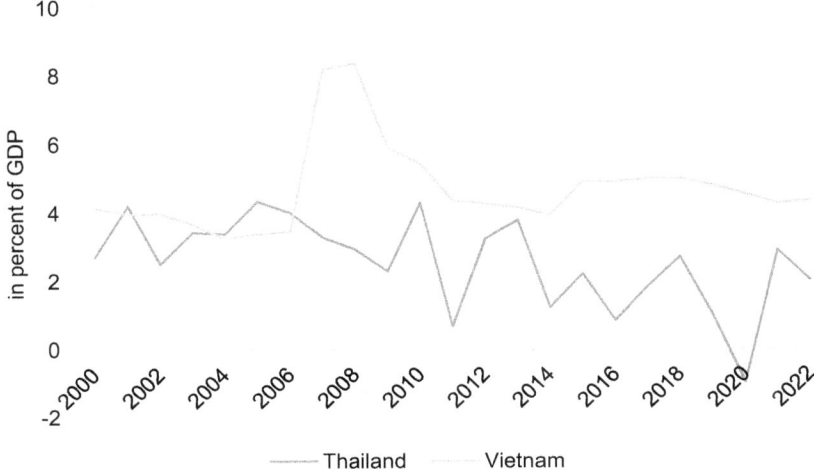

Figure 11 Foreign direct investment inflows as a percentage of GDP in Thailand and Vietnam

Source: Own elaboration based on UNCTAD FDI statistics

regions, such as Eastern Europe and Central America, may lead to promising insights into the intricacies of FDI-based growth. Thailand and Vietnam, in particular, have received vast amounts of direct investment since the 1990s, way above the ECE average. More recently, however, FDI inflows as a percentage of GDP have continued to increase strongly in Vietnam, while having declined in Thailand (Figure 11).

Competition among Southeast Asian countries has been fierce, as other neighboring countries such as Malaysia, Indonesia, and the Philippines are also attracting large volumes of FDI, and high-income economies have proclaimed a geopolitical "pivot to Asia." Key factors for MNCs' investment project decisions are labor costs and the overall political and economic risk, that is, a favorable "business climate" (Pandya, 2016, 462). Having attracted large sums of FDI early on, since the mid-1980s, and having become a relatively advanced economy compared to other countries in the region, Thailand's cost advantage vis-à-vis its competitors has been shrinking over time (OECD, 2021, 96). Consequently, MNCs have gradually relocated operations to neighboring countries such as Vietnam or Cambodia. Adding to this, Thailand's recent history since the mid-2000s is characterized by a series of political crises, social unrest, and two coup d'états in 2006 and 2014, all of which have undermined its investment appeal (Lorch, 2021, 87–9). Dwindling FDI inflows have gradually diminished Thailand's export capacities and competitiveness (Nidhiprabha,

2017). In contrast to its troubled neighbor, Vietnam is considered one of the more politically stable countries in Southeast Asia. In addition to lower production costs, Vietnam has gradually opened its investment regime and has become one of the leading FDI destinations in the region (OECD, 2018b).

Hence, the case of Thailand shows the main problems associated with the FDI-based growth model. First, such a growth model is genuinely dependent on external factors, that is, the investment decisions of multinational corporations. If domestic factors, such as political conflicts or partisan politics, negatively affect the country's status as an investment location, the mid-term sustainability of the model is threatened. Second, one of the key pillars of the model is low production costs, which are eroded by wage growth over time. At some point, MNCs tend to relocate their low-cost operations to other countries. Third, we observe differences in GVC participation across countries, generally captured by the distinction between backward and forward GVC participation. "Backward" participation indicates the degree of foreign inputs in a country's exports, that is, the foreign value-added content of exports. "Forward" participation indicates the degree of a country's domestic value added contained in exports. Whereas forward GVC participation is usually prevalent in commodities and commodity-related sectors, backward GVC participation is highest in simple or advanced manufacturing (Rodrigue, 2024). In contrast to Vietnam, we observe a divergence between backward and forward GVC participation in Thailand in the mid-2000s, with backward participation – involving a potentially higher technology transfer – developing less well (Figure 12).

At the background of the more positive development in Vietnam is the conscious strategy of state authorities to maintain some degree of control over FDI and to extract a substantial transfer of technology in favor of local industry (Lim, 2021). The government has been able to make sure that some value of FDI is retained in the country, in contrast to the more liberal approach in Thailand. Again, we are observing an industrial strategy, which is able to tackle some of the challenges of a dependent integration into GVCs.

In sum, this section has illustrated three types of growth models in the global periphery – commodity-based export-led, debt-based consumption-led, and FDI-based investment-led – that differ fundamentally in terms of the drivers underpinning countries' economic growth and their associated vulnerabilities. However, the paired comparisons within each subtype have revealed substantial heterogeneity. These highlight the potential role of macroeconomic agency in the political management of growth drivers and vulnerabilities, which leads us to examine the importance of the political underpinnings of peripheral growth models.

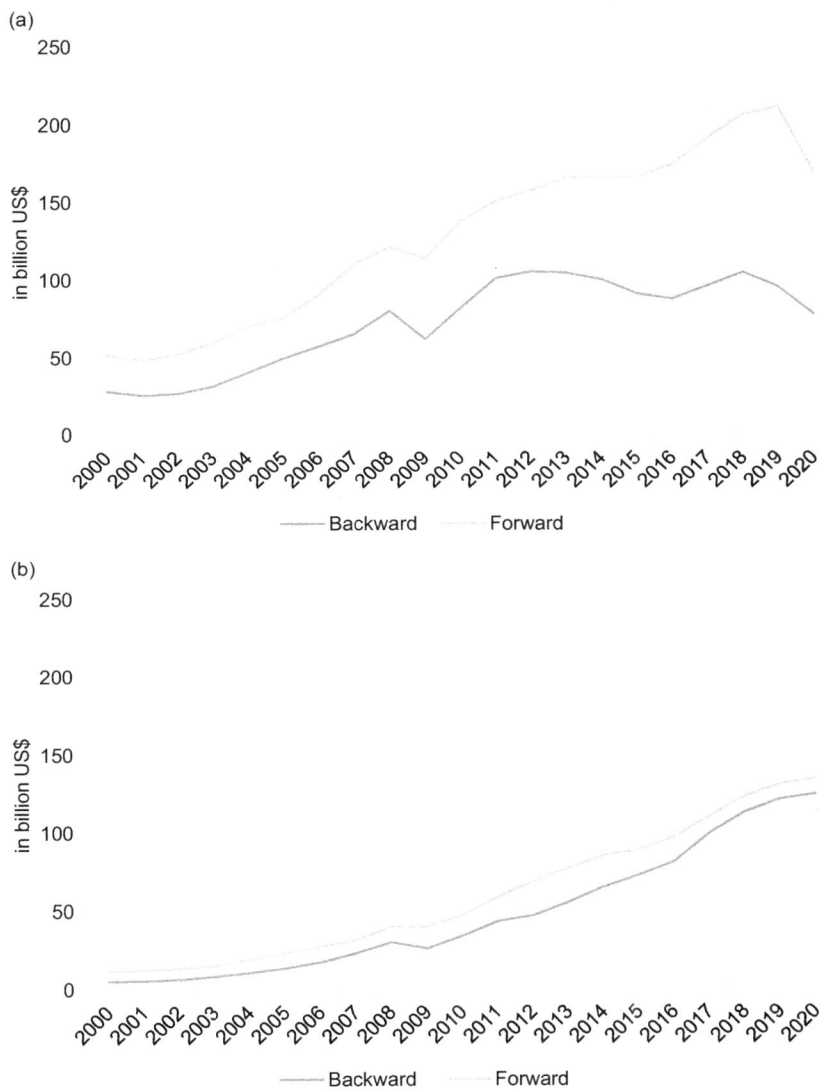

Figure 12 GVC participation of Thailand (a) and Vietnam (b)
Source: Own elaboration based on OECD, Trade in Value-Added database

5 The Political Underpinnings of Peripheral Growth Models

In this section, we focus on the politics of peripheral growth models. In doing so, we counter a narrow view of politics as economic policymaking, highlighting the social and political foundations that are required for growth model stability. We therefore draw on an established body of research on the politics of development

(Section 2.1) and leverage those insights for the GM perspective. In doing so, we aim to go beyond simplistic propositions such as "politics matter." In a nutshell, we argue that the capacity to reduce the external vulnerabilities associated with certain peripheral growth models is related to the political capacity to form broad socio-political support for contested economic policies, especially in times of crises. This capacity, in turn, is facilitated by institutional arrangements, ranging from formal, quasi-corporatist associations to informal patron-client networks.

5.1 The Politics of Peripheral Growth Models

The political support for growth models in ECEs is generally not established via electoral democracy (May et al., 2024). By contrast, the prevalence of the state in many high-growth economies has led to the impression that economic growth in ECEs is "state-directed" (Kohli, 2004).[12] When we see the state not only as a regulator and mediator of political interests, as in the prevalent neo-institutionalist perspective, but also as a source of essential economic resources, its relations to the economic and social environment become important. In fact, there are varying degrees of how strongly the state apparatus is embedded in society (Migdal, 2001). This includes totalitarian or predatory regimes, where the state dictates social relations, and cases of state capture, where the state tends to be an instrument of powerful social groups. The concentration of fiscal resources within the state makes capturing a promising strategy, which leads to higher economic vulnerability (Masi et al., 2024). Therefore, it is crucial that the state displays a certain level of autonomy vis-à-vis demands by social groups, as the developmental state literature has convincingly argued (Evans, 1995).

In what follows, we argue that two factors are crucial to achieve such a "balance of power" between the state and social groups in order to decrease the vulnerability of certain peripheral growth models. First, socioeconomic institutions, such as corporatist arrangements or patron-client networks, serve to include key social interest groups (or stakeholders) to benefit from a particular growth model and compensate excluded groups. Thereby, they help to resolve conflicts among social groups in peaceful ways and promote common over sectional interests (Besley & Persson, 2011). These institutions support, second, the emergence of broad, bipartisan political coalitions which prioritize long-term

---

[12] In fact, some have noted that the expansion of "state capitalism" associated with, among other things, the rise of China, is transforming the global development landscape and its dominant notions of economic policy making (Alami et al., 2021). While we do not have the space to engage substantively with this debate, we believe that the propositions we make may provide a fertile ground for further research into the macroeconomic dimensions of state capitalism research (see also Alami & Dixon, 2020).

investments and institution building over short-term political concerns (Doner & Schneider, 2016). They do this by helping to solve manifold collective action and coordination problems between state actors, businesses, and other social groups such as labor or local power groups (Waldner, 1999).

This contrasts with the widespread view that only impartial institutions, particularly legal ones, are able to bring sustained support to a growth model (see Section 2.1). In contrast, and in line with the political settlements approach, we take a realist stance toward political mediation: patron-client networks can also provide means for political stability and social cohesion. Under certain conditions, they can even increase government effectiveness by resolving principal-agent problems through enhanced monitoring and mutual trust between bureaucrats and politicians (Jiang, 2018; Toral, 2023). Generally, we have to assume that "family," kinship, or the "nation" can also be strong sources of cohesion. In most emerging economies, actors are likely to rely on trust, reciprocity, and loyalty in their economic and political relationships (Maxfield & Schneider, 1997; Amsden, 2001; Witt & Redding, 2013; Nölke et al. 2020; Taylor, 2020). For the analysis of growth models in these contexts, it is therefore important to note that political support does not (necessarily) mean democratic support. Still, relevant actors in the political economy will only support a growth model if they benefit from it.

Consequently, apart from the economic sources of growth (or "growth drivers") covered in Section 3 and the international interdependencies discussed in Section 4, political factors also account for the degree of growth model vulnerability. In fact, they are partly interdependent. Current or historical growth trajectories are likely to shape the productive structure of an economy and the power resources of social groups benefiting from it. As an example, many emerging capitalist economies are characterized by deep structural cleavages between agrarian and financial elites and manufacturing sectors or between domestic business groups and foreign MNCs (Schneider, 2013). Furthermore, religious, ethnic, or spatial cleavages can play out politically and have an effect on growth model stability. These cleavages undermine efforts toward coalition building and can lead to sustained social fragmentation (Doner & Scheider, 2016, 611). Fragmentation, in turn, increases coordination problems between political and economic actors. In particular, in the event of external shocks, such as those emanating from capital outflows or plummeting commodity prices (see Section 4), lacking coordinating capacities becomes a binding constraint for effective policy solutions confronting an unfolding economic crisis. Therefore, we argue that growth models with a broader political and social support, relying on a relatively high degree of elite cohesion, tend to be more stable and resilient toward external shocks.

Our empirical analysis in the subsequent sections calls for a realist view on the politics of growth. Thereby, we aim to move beyond some traditional fault lines in the development discourse. Neither liberal approaches highlighting markets and legal systems, nor statist approaches focusing on bureaucracies and state capacities, are appropriate conceptual frames on their own for analyzing the political and economic realities in the majority of emerging capitalist countries. The political stabilization of a growth model, especially in times of crises, requires the broad political support of crucial social actors whose interests need to be accommodated. In this regard, formal peak associations or informal patron-client networks can intermediate state-business relations successfully and lend support to a given growth model or to a change in growth strategy. Although business associations in emerging economies vary substantially in terms of organizational capacities, they tend to facilitate coordination between their members, other stakeholders, and the state (Doner & Schneider, 2000). Well-organized associations may even contribute to competitiveness and economic growth (Nugent, 2023). As stated, these functions can also potentially be performed by informal state-business relations within elite networks (Nölke et al., 2022). However, the latter are obviously more prone to decay into harmful versions of rent-seeking and corruption.

5.2 The Politics of Export-Led Growth Models

How does the politics of growth models now play out in the different types we presented earlier? To start with, an export-led growth model is in danger of being captured by groups that benefit most from an exclusive access to the sources of export revenues. This is mainly the case when exports are dominated by commodities rather than manufacturing, as there are generally less producer groups involved in raw materials exports than in manufacturing. Consequently, for commodities-based export-led growth models, we observe a high incentive for dominant groups to pursue rent-oriented politics. In order to maintain exclusive access to rents, powerful groups often resort to authoritarian means for the stabilization of the resource-based growth model. This is a well-known feature of many commodities-exporting economies and has been extensively discussed as the "resource curse" (Section 4.1; Ross, 2015). When individual interest groups effectively monopolize the income/rents from growth, strategies for diversifying the growth model and making it more resilient toward exogenous shocks become politically less salient. Therefore, such an export orientation has to be balanced with other sources of growth in order not to endanger the stability of the model.

In contrast to commodities-based models, growth models based on manufacturing exports are more likely to sustain higher growth rates for a longer period of time and are supported by different political settlements. Generally, the South Korean case provides some lessons about the political resilience of manufacturing export-led growth models, despite different historical circumstances: As South Korea's model drew (in the absence of notable commodities) on manufacturing exports, it managed to prevent the capture by groups that would focus on only a few products (Haggard et al., 1991). Old agrarian elites in Korea had lost political power with previous agrarian reforms, and the industrial business groups that emerged in the post-War period were politically weak, at least initially. The state thus was a powerful actor vis-à-vis industrial rent-recipients, making them work in line with industrial upgrading and economic diversification goals (Amsden, 1989; Khan, 2010).[13] The crucial question is how to follow a growth model based on commodity exports that promotes economic diversification, industrial upgrading, and innovation. We argue that politics plays an important role here. Drawing on our case vignettes, we now show how Indonesia has managed to mitigate some vulnerabilities stemming from the commodities-based model politically, while the Brazilian political economy proved to be more vulnerable to political pressure from a coalition between financial capital, agribusiness elites, and the traditional middle class, and therefore deepened its commodity dependence.

From the late 2000s onward, the Indonesian government actively sought to put the commodities sector back under national control, predominantly in the oil, copper, and palm oil sectors (Winanti & Diprose, 2020; Warburton, 2017; 2023). This had two effects: First, the partial exclusion of foreign firms from these sectors increased the power of both the state and domestic businesses; second, natural resources have been actively framed as a case of national sovereignty, particularly in the 2019 election campaign (Winanti & Diprose, 2020, 8). In 2020, the Indonesian commodities sector was more or less in domestic hands again. In this way, the commodities sector plays a crucial role in the common project of Indonesian developmentalism (Warburton, 2023, 181–4). As a national project, it provides a political frame that lends itself to include the majority of relevant stakeholders. Renationalization changed the

---

[13] It is worth noting that developmentalism and industrial upgrading also included labor repression, often brutal, that has escaped benign interpretations such as the ones of the Korean developmental state (Porteux & Kim, 2023). In fact, it has been argued that development state theory more generally has inadequately analyzed regimes of labor control and participation that undergird developmentalist strategies such as import-substitution industrialization (Fishwick, 2019). While we share this perspective and our case illustrations reflect on a wider set of actors, examining the role of labor in different growth trajectories and underlying distributional struggles warrants greater attention than provided here.

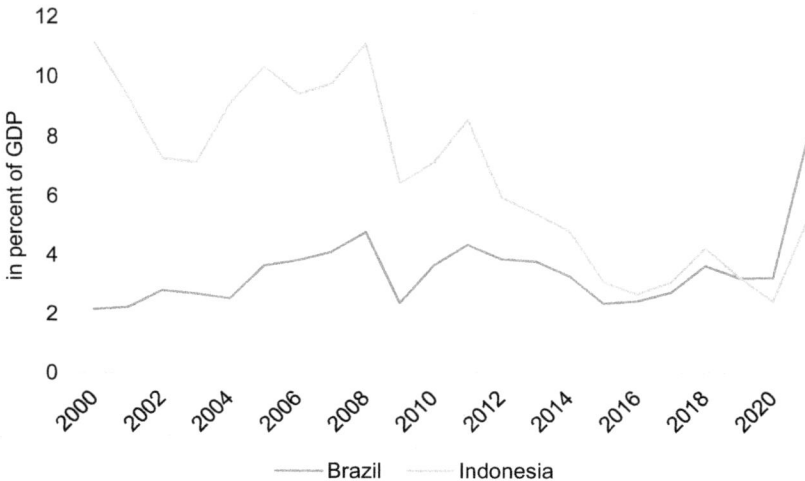

Figure 13 Natural resource rents as a percentage of GDP in Brazil and Indonesia
Source: World Bank Development Indicators

distribution of power among relevant groups, which became represented in a political settlement that stretches across state and business actors. Since natural resources have been framed as a national treasure, it has become hard for particularistic groups to claim exclusive ownership.

Through renationalization, the Indonesian state was able to offer domestic businesses the profit opportunities that hitherto had been exclusively exploited by foreign MNCs (Winanti & Diprose, 2020, 2). In return, the government insisted that domestic business takes part in the resource nationalism program and invest in the domestic economy. At the same time, renationalization changed the contours of the domestic political economy. When commodities had been predominately marketed by foreign MNCs, Indonesia benefited merely in the form of foreign exchange and tax revenues. However, once the earnings of commodities exports flowed into domestic businesses, they would reinvest profits and thus engage in capital accumulation and building relations with up- and downstream businesses, thereby reducing the share of natural resource rents in GDP (Figure 13). Capital accumulation, in turn, also builds on institutions that businesses themselves cannot provide, such as education, credit, and labor legislation. Thus, once commodities became a national endeavor, the number of relevant stakeholders increased. Resource nationalism lent legitimacy to the growth strategy in the wider public and led to interest alignment between key domestic business actors, which proved to benefit from renationalization (Winanti & Diprose, 2020). Although oligarchs and patronage networks are widely accounted for in Indonesia (Fukuoka, 2012; Hadiz & Robison, 2013), these have not led to state capture but to increased competition both within state and private capitalist networks (Pepinsky, 2014; Warburton, 2023, 180–81).

The differences in the Brazilian case are striking. First, the developmentalist project in Brazil halted after 2014 and was mainly framed as a classic case of catch-up industrialization with a higher degree of social justice. Domestic firms were not obliged to invest in forward or backward linkages inside the country, but rather encouraged to internationalize (Ricz & Schedelik, 2023). Consequently, the resource boom did not materialize in a higher degree of capital formation of domestic firms, nor economic diversification. High revenues from commodities exports mainly served to accumulate record levels of international reserves, easing the risk of exchange rate crises (common in the 1990s). Lacking a national project, the usual cleavages in the Brazilian political economy persisted: the strong position of the landowning classes vis-à-vis the poor; Brazilian MNCs enjoying state support for the penetration of world markets vis-à-vis domestic firms aiming for the domestic market; powerful conglomerates vis-à-vis an overall weakly organized business sector (Taylor, 2020; Morgan et al., 2021; Schedelik, 2023, 129–31).

Weak business organization affected the clientelistic favoritism of single firms that sought to further monopolize their influence (May, 2020). For these reasons, they would push for further export specialization rather than diversification. The tight connection between the state and particular firms, especially in commodity-related sectors, led to a situation in which the ruling coalition became ever more dependent on firm support via campaign donations or bribes and kickbacks, leading to ever-increasing rent payments (Schedelik, 2023, 108). Importantly, firms involved in this dynamic typically did not belong to high-value-added manufacturing. Whereas the state in Indonesia was able to urge domestic firms to support a resource nationalist strategy, the political mediation in Brazil became less diversified and more dependent on the state-owned oil company Petrobrás and on large corporations in the construction sector. This Petrobrás-construction nexus became a steadily growing allocator of rents, with ever more groups enjoying rents fueled by windfall profits (Taylor, 2020).

In the absence of competitive pressures from other firms or a stronger transmission of revenues into capital formation and technological upgrading, the incentive to further push for extractivism became ever stronger, minimizing state autonomy vis-à-vis firms and making the commodity-based growth model ultimately unsustainable. The coalition behind extractivism has been too small to actually stabilize the whole growth model politically (Morgan et al., 2021). Brazilian developmentalism has been short-lived and never became a collective project, neither among business nor in the wider public. Widespread skepticism about self-interested elites intensified particularly after the "*lava jato*" corruption scandals (Nölke et al., 2022, 324). When the *lava jato* investigations uncovered the vast corruption schemes involving the PT and many of its allies, the parts of the growth coalition that relied heavily on the Petrobrás-construction nexus virtually imploded. Ultimately, the fragmentation of the coalition, alongside global turbulence, undermined the stability of an existing growth path, giving way to the subsequent right-wing governments of Temer and Bolsonaro, who ran on a neoliberal platform (Morgan et al., 2021, 547).

Clientelism reigns both in Indonesia and Brazil (Epstein, 2009; Sugiyama et al., 2013; Aspinall, 2014; Aspinall & Berenschot, 2019; Power & Rodrigues-Silveira, 2019). Both countries are by no means poster children for a politically efficient export-led model, as we know from the state autonomy literature (Evans, 1995; Kohli, 2004). In contrast to earlier prevalent theories of economic development (Section 2.1), however, the growth model approach also accounts for the less-than-perfect cases where the rule of law, property rights, and impartial bureaucracy are not necessarily granted. In this realist perspective, patronage can equally serve as a means to establish cohesion, especially when the circles of relevant stakeholders become larger and closely connected to the production of higher value-added tradable goods. While important groups have managed to form a political settlement in Indonesia, they have further intensified confrontation in Brazil.

Indonesia, thus, is a case that defies the notion of a resource curse or patrimonial capitalism in some Arab countries (see also Gellert, 2019; Hilmawan & Clark, 2019; on patrimonial capitalism, see Schlumberger, 2008). The Indonesian growth model is not about resource rents all the way down. This means that even within a commodity-based export-led model, there is room for maneuver for a strategy that is not excessively dependent on export revenues, which are vulnerable to fluctuations. It also means that such a growth model is not doomed to get stuck in wasteful rent-seeking in the commodity sector, where export revenues are fueling a clientelist regime, making it politically vulnerable because crucial groups are naturally excluded from those rents. Moreover, the Indonesian case highlights how a political economy with both state- and privately owned firms in the commodities sector is able to support a developmentalist, that is, long-term program. It also shows that states, even if they do not have high levels of state capacities, such as in China, are able to limit the influence of foreign capital. Such a constraining policy toward FDI can have mobilizing effects for domestic capital, which solidifies an otherwise highly volatile sector (for the Chinese case, see Gomes & ten Brink, 2023).

5.3 The Politics of Consumption-Led Growth Models

A consumption-led growth model is potentially threatened by groups that aim to expand (external) debt, thereby increasing the exposure to volatile capital flows (Section 4.2). Through resorting to external debt, it is possible to fuel consumption-led growth without actually having to promote sustainable gains in workers' income through wage increases. Special interest groups, mainly from the finance and real estate sectors, can push such a model, without incorporating other important social groups, such as workers and the poor. Such a strategy requires political resources, but is often easier than organizing broad social compromises, which also involve sharing the revenues of the model among a broader social base. Hence, if a consumption-led model tilts too heavily toward external debt in foreign currency, it becomes vulnerable to fluctuations in international currency markets. Subsequently, we draw on the Turkish and South African case vignettes to show how political dynamics in the former helped to stabilize and diversify a faltering growth model. By contrast, entrenched financial and mining interests locked-in a failed growth model in the latter, leading to crisis and stagnation.

For similar reasons that made Indonesia more stable than Brazil, the political support for balancing Turkey's growth model has been stronger than in South Africa. Again, both countries are far from perfect examples of sustainable economic development, but this is precisely why one can learn from their experience. Like Indonesia, Turkey learned its lessons from severe financial crises and sought to limit the external financial vulnerabilities, for example, by crafting national economic projects. "Anatolian capital" or "Islamic capitalism" have been only two economic "identities" that unified a range of political and economic actors throughout the 2000s (Demir et al., 2004; Demiralp, 2009; Balikci, 2015). Organized capital, labor, and broad segments of voters from multiethnic and various socioeconomic backgrounds supported the Justice and Development Party (AKP), following its first election in 2002 (Apaydin, 2025, 360).

More substantial, however, has been the structure of the Turkish business sector. The Turkish economy is characterized by small and medium enterprises rather than a few powerful national giants (Topal, 2019, 221). As we saw previously, the dominance of a few large companies tends to increase instability because they (mostly domestic MNCs) hardly represent a broad range of groups or sectors and usually are able to pull exit options if necessary. The concentration of bargaining power in such large MNCs leaves too many groups unrepresented in a growth model, particularly when states follow pro-business politics, heavily catering toward a few well-connected firms.

In Turkey, we do not observe such a dominance but rather a relatively effective business organization through associations. Not only do they represent important groups along economic and political cleavages, but they are also particularly powerful in their capacity to organize resources. The Union of Chambers and Commodity Exchanges of Turkey (TOBB), for instance, is representative for a large part of the SME[14] sector but is, at the same time, a peak association that provides crucial resources to both state and business. As Özel (2015, 138) summarizes, it

> lends to the state whenever the state needs it, sponsors large-scale public projects, provides credits and other services for the SMEs, and funds a prominent university and a think-tank, besides representing business interests vis-à-vis the state—and at times vis-à-vis foreign capital. TOBB has invested in a broad range of areas that the private sector eschewed, such as the provision of funds for credit guarantees, storages, renovation of customs offices, etc. The organization often operates like a state agency undertaking state-like functions, and at other times a consultancy firm that provides data and expertise for domestic and international investors.

Hence, it is difficult for the state to ignore its preferences while at the same time, it urges larger firms to join in the domestic economic project. Other associations, such as TÜSİAD, represent big business in a secular orientation, while MÜSİAD would call for a stronger Islamic foundation for the Turkish economy (Yavuz, 2010; Buğra & Savaskan, 2014, 125). Thus, business associations function not only as powerful organizations, but also as key political actors, representing both businesses and wider political orientations. These and other major business organizations across sectoral lines lent substantial support to the government and its growth strategy (Apaydin, 2025, 361–2). However, in the course of the 2010s, this broad supporting coalition declined substantially, especially in light of Erdogan's authoritarian turn from 2013 onward. Following the attempted coup of 2016, authoritarianism was further consolidated. Still, key business groups in the manufacturing, construction, and energy sectors, as well as influential segments of the Islamist middle classes and workers, endorsed the government's shift toward a more diversified growth model, based on an industrial strategy and export promotion (Akcay & Jungmann, 2023, 553–4; Apaydin, 2025, 363–7).

---

[14] Small and medium-sized enterprise.

Still, we observe a diversified representation of economic and political interests that amounted to a stable balance of power between state and business for the better part of the 2000s and early 2010s in Turkey. A large part of domestic consumption took place in the construction sector (Erol, 2019), which in turn involved crucial stakeholders: the state, large domestic construction businesses, and domestic banks. In this form, construction remained a Turkish business because neither foreign firms have been significantly involved in construction nor is retail investment significantly connected to foreign capital markets. It comes as no surprise that the construction sector, where multiple interests can be found, is a major site of clientelist networks (Sayarı, 2014, 11). However, these networks can be interpreted as means of coordination and compliance rather than purely rent-seeking. Similar to Indonesia, we see the co-existence of patronage and stable political settlements. As neither the state nor major businesses is able to monopolize power, patronage and clientelist networks have been able to include a growing number of relevant stakeholders, thereby mitigating the withdrawal of support by some social groups (Sayarı, 2014, 11; Apaydin, 2025).

In South Africa, in turn, the political foundation for a sustainable debt-based consumption-led growth model has been far more unstable. At first, it has been far more transnationally integrated than the Turkish one, leading to a much higher degree of vulnerability from volatile financial markets (Isaacs & Kaltenbrunner, 2018; Karwowski, 2018; Ansari, 2021). Second, the South African state is not powerful enough to garner widespread support for a more diversified growth model or inhibit crucial actors to draw exit-options: Foreign firms and banks are players in the political bargains over the growth model (which they are not in Turkey or Indonesia), at the same time, large domestic businesses have exit-options since they have long established transnational corporate relations (Karwowski, 2015). The large South African mining MNCs are neither dependent on nor interested in submitting to a national growth project but follow particularistic agendas (Chipkin & Swilling, 2018; Claar, 2018; Bowman, 2020). In addition, the powerful financial sector, with its strong ties to the Treasury and the Central Bank, has been highly successful in blocking alternative growth strategies, even in the wake of the global financial crisis. Those alternative industrial strategies were promoted by leftist factions of the African National Congress and the major trade unions but failed to alter the prevailing debt-based model (Naqvi, 2023, 301–7).

Third, racial cleavages still represent a deep rift in the South African political economy, one of the most unequal countries globally. As an example, the promotion of Black Economic Empowerment seeks for completely different plans on how to organize the economy as a whole, contesting highly unequal and racialized ownership structures of farm land in particular. Instead of a diversification of stakeholders, South Africa is rather characterized by a high degree of fragmentation, where capitalist factions cannot settle on the common support for growth models (Bowman, 2019). Of course, clientelism and patronage are also widespread in South Africa, but here it takes the form of monopolistic rent-seeking, which typically prevents economic diversification and industrial upgrading. Just like Petrobrás in Brazil, the national electricity giant ESKOM served as the main source and distributor for rents (Ansari, 2021, 172). When ESKOM got into trouble, the flow of rents diminished, and so did the compliance of beneficiaries. Political coordination as a whole, therefore, is weak, amplified by the persistence of racial hierarchy and state violence in the resolution of labor disputes (such as in the Marikana massacre during a miners' strike).

To sum up, the higher vulnerability of the South African debt-based growth model toward global financial cycles in comparison to the Turkish one (see Section 4.2) is also based on its much more fragmented political support base. Neither state nor business is powerful enough to establish a common and coherent alternative growth strategy. In Turkey, in contrast, the AKP-led government had been able to assemble a broad support base for its growth strategy throughout the 2000s and early 2010s, also comprising of small enterprises and a large share of households. Although this broad support was gradually weakened in light of rising authoritarianism by the end of the decade, it helped to stabilize and diversify a faltering debt-based model.

5.4 The Politics of Investment-Led Growth Models

Finally, an investment-led model has distributional implications as well, which highlights the importance of the political support coalitions underpinning this model. Investments can come from external as well as from internal sources. An excessive orientation on foreign investments, however, raises the vulnerability of the growth model because foreign owners are more likely to divest funds when conditions allow.

It is difficult to speak of capture properly in this case, but this kind of danger also applies to investment-led growth models. Some social groups and political elites have a high interest in attracting FDI: FDI is usually indicative of a promising manufacturing industry, it eases the balance of payment constraint, and comes with no strings attached in a political sense, as no social group suffers from a relocation of investments, at least initially (Owen, 2018). Hence, from a political perspective, FDI can be seen as a form of rent (Pinto & Zhu, 2022; Brazys et al., 2023), which will increasingly define the whole growth model and, eventually, the entire political economy can become heavily dependent on FDI (Bohle & Regan, 2021). Indeed, a large share of FDI in some sectors can lead to a crowding out of investments by domestic groups, typically less resourceful than large MNCs. Moreover, even considering the positive effects of MNCs' productive investments – those investments that most relevant groups in an economy welcome – over time, the share of portfolio investments may grow as a strategy to keep the balance of payments in check.

At this point, such a foreign-dominated investment-led model becomes vulnerable for at least three reasons: First, in the absence of capital controls, capital that flows in easily often flows out easily as well, especially when we are dealing with large volumes of portfolio capital that is highly mobile. Second, the different domestic economic groups in an FDI-dependent economy are not essentially part of the growth model but merely pacified. As research on the Eastern European economies has shown, foreign chambers of commerce and large foreign investors play an outsized role in shaping and sustaining this type of growth model (Scheiring, 2020; Bohle & Regan, 2021). Hence, broader political support for an FDI-led growth model often relies on the promised spillover effects of FDI inflows for growth, innovation, jobs, and tax revenues, which usually remain on a rather abstract scale and are yet to materialize. This means that the political support for an FDI-led model is rather fragile because the costs for most actors to exit the model are relatively low. Thirdly, FDI dependency usually goes together with policies to attract FDI. These policies involve direct (e.g., subsidies) and indirect transfers (e.g., tax exemptions) to foreign corporations – which open the gate for distributional conflicts.

Again, the two cases discussed in the context of international interdependencies are instructive in this regard (Section 4.3). Thailand has a recent history of political instability, thereby discouraging MNC investment. At least as important is the loss of labor cost advantages on the side of Thailand, vis-à-vis neighboring countries such as Vietnam. Finally, Thailand relies on the voluntary transfer of innovations by MNCs, thereby increasing the probability of remaining stuck in a middle-income trap. Vietnam, in contrast, has been developing institutions with the objective of ensuring that investments by MNCs involve technology transfer toward the domestic industry (Klingler-Vidra & Wade, 2020). In fact, Thailand has followed an open inward investment policy since the 1980s already. As mentioned earlier, in contrast to portfolio investments, greenfield investments usually come with technology, management innovation, and integration into international production networks. Yet, any productive effect of FDI requires appropriate "absorptive capacities" (Cohen & Levinthal, 1990) in the host country, which are mainly missing in Thailand. As Thailand never had a substantial industrial or technology policy, foreign investment could not increase the capacities of domestic firms, which has led to hardly any developmental impact (Kanchoochat et al., 2021, 16).

Vietnam, in contrast, represents a gradual process of market opening (Ngo & Tarko, 2018). The introduction of market principles from the 1980s onward did not follow a prefigured plan set by the communist party (Gainsborough, 2017, 136). Therefore, Vietnam is far from the ideal-typical developmental state that is able to both make grand development plans and implement them through an effective bureaucracy. The evolving state-business relation can rather be understood as a form of "hybrid corporatism" (Nguyen, 2014, 338). This has worked because business has some degree of organizational power and therefore could establish peak associations. Unlike the dirigiste model of coordination as it is found in traditional developmental state regimes, associations are potentially helpful in managing the diverse interests that arise in processes of societal and economic fragmentation. Local businesses, political cleavages, and a fragmented state do not call for a political model of a strong state (Gainsborough, 2017; Pincus, 2023). Both the ambitions and strategies of the state and business are changing constantly, and such an intermediation is able to accommodate the changing alliances that go along with it.

Informal mechanisms of coordination play an important role as well. However, these are not mere instruments for the appropriation of monopolistic rents but help to include a range of actors in a common political project. Although less salient today, a blend of socialism and economic nationalism still serves as an important ideological framework that large parts of Vietnamese society can adhere to (London, 2022, 36–7). From this perspective, the "Vietnam example ... illustrates that a crony capitalist growth path could enable growth and development, thanks to the interplay between politics, institutions, and markets, despite the lack of universal rule of law as well as contract and property protection" (Ngo & Tarko, 2018, 15). Similar to the case of Turkey, we observe a productive kind of clientelism.

Many of the elements that helped to stabilize the Vietnamese growth model politically have been absent in Thailand. There has been no common growth or development project that could serve as a political umbrella. However, what is even more important are stable procedures of building societal coalitions, reliable mechanisms of coordination or accommodation, and non-monopolistic relations of power. In these respects, Thailand is much more unstable and imbalanced. Unlike Vietnam or Turkey, we neither find effective associations that would act as corporate actors mediating between state and business nor other significant institutionalized forms of state-business relations (Doner & Schneider, 2016, 633). Like in Brazil or South Africa, large corporations have substantial political influence, following particularistic interests.

Under such circumstances, including an unstable polity, the risk of monopolistic rent absorption is high. The Thai economy is dominated by a small number of families and their conglomerates. Through their preferred access to the state (e.g., via receiving licenses), these groups could grow exponentially compared to the average growth in the country (Kanchoochat et al., 2021, 17). We find a broad stratification, where elites compete for power and resources at the top, while poverty increases at the bottom. Politically, Thailand is highly fragile: Instead of common growth projects, we have observed two coups d'état within ten years (2006 and 2014). Added to the "usual" competing elites of state and business, military elites – who pursue their own economic interests – complicate the situation even further. Deep cleavages and open conflicts between supporters of former Prime Minister Thaksin Shinawatra (2001–2006) and his adversaries have marked the Thai polity for two decades, leading to a highly vulnerable authoritarian coalition ruling the country since 2014 (Sen & Tyce, 2019, 131–2). As one observer put it, "[a] lack of consensus around basic 'rules of the game' among elites and civil societal groups renders the country highly volatile and unstable" (Kongkirati, 2016, 17). In this context, it should come as no surprise that stable support for a particular growth model is hard to achieve.

In conclusion, associations are a central counterpart for the state as well as a representative for their constituency. Their establishment goes hand in hand with organizational professionalization because, as main negotiators, they have to move beyond particularistic interests. As we know from established corporatist systems, associations represent a crucial element in the coordination of different interests, therefore contributing to the process of accommodation between businesses as well as between state and business. Whether they use formal or informal channels of coordination does not really matter here. What matters is that the political stabilization of a growth model rests on a broad support where crucial actors cannot defect easily. If we look at our case vignettes, we can see that the less vulnerable economies (Indonesia, Turkey, and Vietnam) have peak associations while they play a very little, if any, role in Brazil, South Africa, and Thailand. Although we would not go as far as to say that associations are key to the stabilization of growth models, their existence seems to have a positive effect. They indicate the existence of some level of intermediation between state and business, which helps to foster elite cohesion and to solve manifold coordination problems, in particular in times of crises.

More generally, we have shown that political support is a crucial factor for the stability of a growth model and the mitigation of its external vulnerabilities. Through our analysis of a small number of cases, we are starting to be able to specify which political conditions have to be met and which aspects are analytically less important. Broad support for a growth model adds to its stability, especially under conditions of high vulnerability: When state-business relations are not monopolized by a few large firms, it reduces the risk that these actors exit a given growth coalition and opt for a different strategy. Similarly, it is harder for these actors to lock-in an unstable growth model, thereby increasing the vulnerabilities that arise when economies become too dependent on commodity exports, external debt, and FDI inflows.

6 Conclusion and Perspectives

In this Element, we have demonstrated how an adapted growth model perspective can help to unpack divergent growth trajectories and sources of uneven economic development. More specifically, we have indicated how the GM perspective is able to complement existing political economy approaches to economic development. We argue that this approach provides an alternative to universalizing economic models and policies prevalent in some areas of development discourse, both of the neo-institutionalist and the developmental-statist variety. In particular, we contend that it is able to better incorporate economic agency and state-business relations, not least to point out the policy leeway that is available, especially for large emerging capitalist economies. To this end, we pursued three objectives.

First, we have expanded the existing GM approach, conventionally applied to advanced capitalist countries in the OECD, in order to assist us in understanding emerging capitalist economies. We have developed a novel and coherent typology of peripheral growth models for emerging capitalist economies. Among the important contributions of this typology is the depiction of two different types of investment-led growth models, based on the distinction between domestic and foreign sources of investment. We have grounded this typology in macroeconomic data on large emerging economies for the period between 2001 and 2022, demonstrating that these economies pursue quite different growth models based on contributions to aggregate demand.

Second, we have expanded existing discussions on growth models in CPE by highlighting that the international context for these growth models is different from that in the OECD world. More specifically, we have mobilized research from development studies to demonstrate that peripheral growth models are subject to specific vulnerabilities, that is, commodity export-led growth models to commodity cycles, debt-led models to fluctuations of financial flows, and FDI-led growth models to relocation decisions by multinational corporations. At the same time, we have shown – via paired comparisons – that state-business orchestration of national growth strategies can make a substantial difference when dealing with these vulnerabilities.

Third, we have demonstrated that the different types of export-, consumption-, and investment-led growth models each have their specific vulnerabilities regarding the political support base required for the stabilization of these. Again, these types of political coalitions and state-business relations differ quite considerably from the pattern observed by research on growth models in OECD economies. Overall, we have highlighted that the establishment of broad political coalitions, enhanced by the existence of peak associations, are particularly effective for reducing the vulnerabilities of different growth models. In contrast, narrower coalitions focusing on ones focusing on the short-term gains of those social groups which benefit most from these models (e.g., large agricultural or mining companies in the case of commodity-based export-led growth).

Given the scope of this Element, our brief vignettes on Brazil, Indonesia, South Africa, Thailand, Turkey, and Vietnam could only provide an illustrative and cursory treatment of these three contributions. They were instrumental to the objective of proposing an empirical research program in development studies, grounded on concepts and debates from CPE, but far from sufficient historical-comparative analyses. Future research on peripheral growth models thus needs to investigate in greater detail how emerging capitalist economies instigate, reproduce, or change growth models and how their political bases deal with the vulnerabilities emerging from their kind of growth. Given the specific vulnerabilities of each of the three types of growth models, one objective may be to seek out for mixed types, where a combination of growth drivers assists in reducing the vulnerabilities incurred by dependency on only one growth driver. For example, we could speak of a *domestic demand-led growth model* if private consumption, government consumption, and investment together contribute relatively equally to output growth. As there are various growth drivers and components of aggregate demand playing an important role, the level of vulnerability would be relatively low in this mixed type. A *balanced growth model*, in turn, would represent a situation when all components of aggregate demand contribute roughly the same to GDP growth. Even more than in the domestic demand-led model, a balanced growth model should exhibit lower levels of potential vulnerability than any of the models introduced in this Element.

Moreover, future research may devote greater attention to the classical question of who benefits from what kind of growth, thereby complementing our focus on the stability and vulnerability of growth models. Although the original discussion on growth models in CPE (Baccaro & Pontusson, 2016) paid considerable attention to earnings inequality and income distribution, this focus has largely gone missing in the subsequent debate. For the study of ECE economies, however, the study of distributional implications might be of heightened importance. For instance, the finding that commodity-based growth models can at least temporarily stimulate broad-based domestic consumption stands in stark contrast to established findings that heavy commodity dependence negatively affects economic equality (Nkurunziza et al., 2017; Natanael, 2025).

Another avenue for future research, thus, would be to combine the two dominant strands of CPE for the study of economic development, given that at least some strands of the institutionalist supply-side research program paid attention to issues of inequality (Bizberg, 2019; Nölke et al., 2020). The identification of growth models – and the analysis of their interactions with various types of international interdependencies – focuses on the macroeconomic (demand) side of the economy and on economic policies. As we have shown, the development of the GM perspective in CPE was a conscious attempt to break with the previous focus of the VoC approach on supply-side institutions (Baccaro and Pontusson, 2016, 181). However, this turn may have been too radical, especially for the study of emerging economies. First, institutions matter considerably for the success of some growth models, as, for example, manufacturing-based growth requires institutional complementarities for specific types of innovations (Nölke, 2021). Second, the potential option to switch between growth models – or at least to balance one-sided growth models – leads to the question of which type of macroeconomic and social institutions are most conducive to this kind of maneuver.

Such a research endeavor could, in fact, find more common ground with the neo-institutionalist and statist approaches in development studies and thus could contribute to the emergence of a more robust framework for understanding development and growth. In doing so, such a framework could also reflect on the limitations of the GM perspective as proposed in this Element. For one, this refers to the sometimes-functionalist rationalizations of aggregate macroeconomic data and distributive struggles. Acknowledging historical contingencies will only become more important as peripheral economies have to navigate the stormy weather of global economic re-ordering. Development trajectories are often shaped by geopolitical circumstances, and neither the VoC nor the GM perspective have reflected this in their analytical apparatus. As geopolitical competition may lead to the diversion of investment in certain sectors or regions, or may create barriers to trade and investment more generally, designing effective development and growth strategies structured around specific demand components must respond to the associated vulnerabilities. Moreover, the current global conjecture – triggered in particular by the second Trump government and emergent features of bloc confrontation – may also mean that the implicit assumption of a higher degree of stability in non-peripheral growth models has to be revisited, given that the latter also show an increasing degree of vulnerability. At the same time, new geopolitical frictions may create novel conditions for peripheral growth trajectories and, indeed, allow for structural upgrading beyond the short-to-mid-term perspective presented here.

Finally, a different blind spot identified for the first wave of GM research has been the persistent dominance of the growth paradigm and the ignorance of climate or planetary crisis in its analytical grasp (Green, 2022). For the sake of the argument, this Element has not rectified this shortcoming. Developmental outcomes are so much more than economic growth rates and aggregate demand compositions. But even within the narrow focus that is provided by GM research, adjustments are needed. First of all, different growth models have different implications for environmental sustainability. For example, a growth model reliant on resource extraction contributes more to environmental degradation, but may be interdependent with green growth strategies in capitalist core economies. Second, peripheral economies are, generally speaking, much more vulnerable to climate change and, in part for reasons of external indebtedness and weak fiscal resources, less capable of mitigating and adapting. Understanding the interconnections between the economic and political dimensions of peripheral growth models and their climate- and non-climate vulnerabilities is therefore of utmost importance for decades to come. There is no reason why CPE and development studies should tackle this on separate pathways.

References

Acemoglu, D. (2025). Institutions, technology and prosperity. *NBER Working Paper* 33442. www.nber.org/system/files/working_papers/w33442/w33442.pdf [accessed 4 April 2025].

Acemoglu, D. & Robinson, J. A. (2012). *Why Nations Fail: The Origins of Power, Prosperity, and Poverty*. New York, NY: Crown.

Acemoglu, D., Johnson, S. & Robinson, J. A. (2005). Institutions as a fundamental cause of long-run growth. In P. Aghion and S. N. Durlauf, eds., *Handbook of Economic Growth*, Volume 1, Part A. Amsterdam: North-Holland, pp. 385–472.

Aghion, P. & Howitt, P. (2009). *The Economics of Growth*. Cambridge, MA: The MIT Press.

Ahuja, A. & Nabar, M. (2012). Investment-led growth in China: Global spillovers. *IMF Working Papers* No 2012/267. www.imf.org/external/pubs/ft/wp/2012/wp12267.pdf [accessed 4 April 2025].

Akcay, Ü. & Güngen, A. R. (2022). Dependent financialisation and its crisis: The case of Turkey. *Cambridge Journal of Economics*, 46(2), 293–316.

Akcay, U. & Jungmann, B. (2023). Growth regimes, dominant social blocs and growth strategies: Towards varieties of export-led growth regimes and strategies in Turkey and Poland. *European Journal of Economics and Economic Policies: Intervention*, 20(3), 539–60.

Akcay, Ü., Hein, E. & Jungmann, B. (2022). Financialisation and macroeconomic regimes in emerging capitalist economies before and after the great recession. *International Journal of Political Economy*, 51(2), 77–100.

Akyüz, Y. (2022). The commodity-finance nexus: Twin boom and double whammy. *Revista de Economia Contemporânea*, 24(1), 1–13.

Alami, I., Alves, C., Bonizzi, B., et al. (2023). International financial subordination: A critical research agenda. *Review of International Political Economy*, 30(4), 1360–86.

Alami, I. & Dixon, A. (2020). State capitalism(s) redux? Theories, tensions, controversies. *Competition & Change*, 24(1), 70–94.

Alami, I., Dixon, A. & Mawdsley, E. (2021). State capitalism and the new global D/development regime. *Antipode*, 53(5), 1294–318.

Alenda-Demoutiez, J. (2022). From economic growth to the human: Reviewing the history of development visions over time and moving forward. *Third World Quarterly*, 43(5), 1038–55.

References

Amable, B. & Palombarini, S. (2024). The concept of the social bloc in political economy. *Political Economy Working Papers*, No. 4/2024. University of Geneva.

Amable, B., Regan, A., Avdagic, S., et al. (2019). New approaches to political economy. *Socio-Economic Review*, 17(2), 433–59.

Amsden, A. H. (1989). *Asia's Next Giant: South Korea and Late Industrialization*. Oxford: Oxford University Press.

Amsden, A. H. (2001). *The Rise of "The Rest": Challenges to the West from Late-Industrializing Economies*. New York, NY: Oxford University Press.

Ansari, S. (2021). *Neoliberalism and Resistance in South Africa: Economic and Political Coalitions*. Cham: Palgrave Macmillan.

Antràs, P. (2020). Conceptual aspects of global value chains. *The World Bank Economic Review*, 34(3), 551–74.

Apaydin, F. (2025). Repression and growth in the periphery of Europe: The politics of changing growth regime in Turkey. *Competition & Change*, 29(3–4), 352–74.

Apaydin, F. & Çoban, M. K. (2023). The political consequences of dependent financialization: Capital flows, crisis and the authoritarian turn in Turkey. *Review of International Political Economy*, 30(3), 1046–72.

Arnold, C. & Adnan N. (2024). Seeking autonomy in the semi-periphery: Neomercantilism and diversification in Turkey. *Studies in Comparative International Development*, 59, 665–89.

Aspinall, E. (2014). When brokers betray: Clientelism, social networks, and electoral politics in Indonesia. *Critical Asian Studies*, 46(4), 545–70.

Aspinall, E. & Berenschot, W. (2019). *Democracy for Sale: Elections, Clientelism, and the State in Indonesia*. Ithaca, NY: Cornell University Press.

Avlijaš, S. & Gartzou-Katsouyanni, K. (2024). Firm-centered approaches to overcoming semi-peripheral constraints. *Studies in Comparative International Development*, 59(4), 611–35.

Avlijaš, S. & Gartzou-Katsouyanni, K. (2025). Firms and economic development in the semi-periphery. In M. Regini, ed., *Handbook of Comparative Political Economy*. Oxford: Oxford University Press, pp. 392–410.

Avlijaš, S., Hassel, A. & Palier, B. (2021). Growth strategies and welfare reforms in Europe. In A. Hassel and B. Palier, eds., *Growth and Welfare in Advanced Capitalist Economies: How Have Growth Regimes Evolved?* Oxford: Oxford University Press, pp. 372–436.

Ay, A., Akar, G. & Akar, T. (2016). Middle income trap: A comparison between BRICS countries and Turkey. *Economic and Environmental Studies*, 16(2), 279–301.

Baccaro, L., Blyth, M. & Pontusson, J., eds., (2022). *Diminishing Returns: The New Politics of Growth and Stagnation*. Oxford: Oxford: University Press.

Baccaro, L. & Hadziabdic, S. (2024). Operationalizing growth models. *Quality & Quantity*, 58, 1325–60.

Baccaro, L. & Hadziabdic, S. (2025). Elective Affinities: The Sectoral Underpinnings of Growth Models. Unpublished manuscript.

Baccaro, L. & Pontusson, J. (2016). Rethinking comparative political economy: The growth model perspective. *Politics and Society*, 44(2), 175–207.

Baccaro, L. & Pontusson, J. (2018). Comparative political economy and varieties of macroeconomics. *MPIfG Discussion Paper* 18/10. Cologne: Max Planck Institute for the Study of Societies.

Baldwin, R. (2016). *The Great Convergence: Information Technology and the New Globalization*. Cambridge, MA: Harvard University Press.

Balikci, E. (2015). Turkey's small capital, a player from the start: relations with the state and big capital. *Enterprise & Society*, 16(1), 74–108.

Ban, C. & Adascalitei, D. (2022). The FDI-led growth models of the East-Central and South-Eastern European periphery. In M. Blyth, J. Pontusson, and L. Baccaro, eds., *Diminishing Returns: The New Politics of Growth and Stagnation*. Oxford: Oxford University Press, pp. 189–211.

Banerjee, A. V. & Duflo, E. (2019). *Good Economics for Hard Times: Better Answers to Our Biggest Problems*. London: Allen Lane.

Bauerle Danzmann, S., Wincoff, W. K. & Oatley, T. (2017). All crises are global: Capital cycles in an imbalanced international political economy. *International Studies Quarterly*, 61(4), 907–23.

Becker, U., ed., (2013). *The BRICs and Emerging Economies in Comparative Perspective: Political Economy, Liberalisation and Institutional Change*. London: Routledge.

Becker, U. & Vasileva, A. (2017). Russia's political economy re-conceptualised: A changing hybrid of liberalism, statism and patrimonialism. *Journal of Eurasian Studies*, 8(1), 83–96.

Behuria, P. (2025). Donors and disciplines meet the political economy of development: The contested evolution of political settlements analysis. *Progress in Development Studies*, online first.

Besley, T. & Persson, T. (2011). *Pillars of Prosperity: The Political Economics of Development Clusters*. Princeton, NJ: Princeton University Press.

Bizberg, I. (2019). *Diversity of Capitalisms in Latin America*. Houndmills: Palgrave Macmillan.

Blecker, R. & Setterfield, M. (2019). *Heterodox Macroeconomics: Models of Demand, Distribution and Growth*. Cheltenham: Edward Elgar.

Blyth, M. & Matthijs, M. (2017). Black swans, lame ducks, and the mystery of IPE's missing macroeconomy. *Review of International Political Economy*, 24(2), 203–31.

Bohle, D. & Regan, A. (2021). The comparative political economy of growth models: Explaining the continuity of FDI-led growth in Ireland and Hungary. *Politics and Society*, 49(1), 75–106.

Bohle, D. & Regan, A. (2022). Global capital and national growth models: The cases of Ireland and Latvia. In M. Blyth, J. Pontusson and L. Baccaro, eds., *Diminishing Returns: The New Politics of Growth and Stagnation*. Oxford: Oxford University Press, pp. 323–48.

Bondy, A. & Maggor, E. (2024). Balancing the scales: Labour incorporation and the politics of growth model transformation. *New Political Economy*, 29(1), 22–41.

Bonizzi, B., Kaltenbrunner, A. & Powell, J. (2020). Subordinate financialization in emerging capitalist economies. In P. Mader, D. Mertens, and N. van der Zwan, eds., *The Routledge International Handbook of Financialization*. London: Routledge, pp. 177–87.

Bonizzi, B., Kaltenbrunner, A. & Powell, J. (2022): Financialised capitalism and the subordination of emerging capitalist economies. *Cambridge Journal of Economics*, 46(4), 651–78.

Bonizzi, B. & Karwowski, E. (2024). Commonality without convergence: An analytical framework accounting for variegated financialisation in emerging economies. *Competition & Change*, 28(2), 293–317.

Bowman, A. (2019). Black economic empowerment policy and state–business relations in South Africa: The case of mining. *Review of African Political Economy*, 46(160), 223–45.

Bowman, A. (2020). Parastatals and economic transformation in South Africa: The political economy of the Eskom crisis. *African Affairs*, 119(476), 395–431.

Brahmbhatt, M., Canuto, O. & Vostroknutova, E. (2010). Dealing with Dutch disease. *Economic Premise*, June 2010, No 16. Washington, DC.

Brazys, S., de Soysa, I. & Vadlamannati, K. C. (2023). Blessing or curse? Assessing the local impacts of foreign direct investment on conflict in Africa. *Journal of Peace Research*, 62(1), 149–65.

Bresser-Pereira, L.-C. (2020). Neutralizing the Dutch disease. *Journal of Post-Keynesian Economics*, 43(2), 298–316.

Breznitz, D. & Gingrich, J. (2025). Industrial policy revisited. *Annual Review of Political Science*, 28, 329–50.

Briguglio L., Cordina, G., Farrugia, N. & Vella, S. (2009). Economic vulnerability and resilience: Concepts and measurements. *Oxford Development Studies*, 37(3), 229–47.

Buğra, A. & Savaşkan, O. (2012). Politics and class: The Turkish business environment in the neoliberal age. *New Perspectives on Turkey*, 46, 27–63.

Buğra, A. & Savaşkan, O. (2014). *New Capitalism in Turkey*. Cheltenham: Edward Elgar.

Bulfone, F., Madariaga, A. & Tassinari, A. (2025). Introduction: The politics of growth, stagnation and upgrading in peripheral advanced economies. *Competition & Change*, 29(3–4), 295–314.

Camba, A., Lim, G. & Kevin G. (2022). Leading sector and dual economy: How Indonesia and Malaysia mobilised Chinese capital in mineral processing. *Third World Quarterly*, 43(10), 2375–95.

Campana, J. M., Vaz, J. E., Hein, E. & Jungmann, B. (2024). Demand and growth regimes of the BRICs countries – the national income and financial accounting decomposition approach and an autonomous demand-led growth perspective. *European Journal of Economics and Economic Policies*, 22(1), 17–41.

Cardoso, F. E. & Faletto, E. (1979). *Dependency and Development in Latin America*. Berkeley, CA: University of California Press.

Carney, R. W. (2016). Varieties of hierarchical capitalism: Family and state market economies in East Asia. *The Pacific Review*, 29(2), 137–63.

Carstens, A. & Shin, H. S. (2019). Emerging markets aren't out of the woods yet. *Foreign Affairs*, 15 March.

Chang, H.-J. (2011). Institutions and economic development: Theory, policy and history. *Journal of Institutional Economics*, 7(4), 473–98.

Chipkin, I. & Swilling, M. (2018). *Shadow State: The Politics of State Capture*. Johannesburg: Wits University Press.

Claar, S. (2018). *International Trade Policy and Class Dynamics in South Africa: The Economic Partnership Agreement*. Houndmills: Palgrave Macmillan.

Clift, B. (2021). *Comparative Political Economy: States, Markets and Global Capitalism*. 2nd ed., London: Bloomsbury.

Çoban, M. K. & Apaydın, F. (2025). Navigating financial cycles: Economic growth, bureaucratic autonomy, and regulatory governance in emerging markets. *Regulation & Governance*, 19(1), 126–45.

Cohen, W. & Levinthal, D. (1990). Absorptive capacity: A new perspective on learning and innovation. *Administrative Science Quarterly*, 35(1), 128–52.

Corden W. M. (1984). Booming sector and Dutch disease economics: survey and consolidation. *Oxford Economic Papers*, 36(3), 359–80.

Demir, O., Acar, M. & Toprak, M. (2004). Anatolian tigers or Islamic capital: Prospects and challenges. *Middle Eastern Studies*, 40(6), 166–88.

Demiralp, S. (2009). The rise of Islamic capital and the decline of Islamic radicalism in Turkey. *Comparative Politics*, 41(3), 315–35.

De Ville, F. & Vermeiren, M. (2016). The Eurozone crisis and the rise of China in the global monetary and trading system: The political economy of an asymmetric shock. *Comparative European Politics*, 14, 572–603.

Dierckx, S. (2015). *Capital Controls in China, Brazil and India: Towards the End of the free Movement of Capital as a Global Norm?* (PhD dissertation). Ghent: Ghent University.

Doner, R. F. & Schneider, B. R. (2000). Business associations and economic development: Why some associations contribute more than others. *Business and Politics*, 2(3), 261–88.

Doner, R. F. & Schneider, B. R. (2016). The middle-income trap: More politics than economics. *World Politics*, 68(4), 608–44.

Dreher, S. (2015). Islamic capitalism? The Turkish Hizmet business community network in a global economy. *Journal of Business Ethics*, 129(4), 823–32.

Eichengreen, B. & Hausmann, R., eds., (2005). *Other People's Money: Debt Denomination and Financial Instability in Emerging Market Economies*. Chicago, IL: University of Chicago Press.

Epstein, D. J. (2009). Clientelism versus ideology: Problems of party development in Brazil. *Party Politics*, 15(3), 335–55.

Erol, I. (2019). Financial transformation and housing finance in Turkey. In G. L. Yalman, T. Marois and A. R. Güngen, eds., *The Political Economy of Financial Transformation in Turkey*. New York, NY: Routledge, pp. 243–68.

Erten, B. & Ocampo, J. A. (2013). Super cycles of commodity prices since the mid-nineteenth century. *World Development*, 44, 14–30.

Evans, P. (1995). *Embedded Autonomy: States and Industrial Transformation*. Princeton: Princeton University Press.

Evans, P. & Heller, P. (2015). Human development, state transformation and the politics of the developmental state. In S. Leibfried, E. Huber, M. Lange, J. Levy and J. D. Stephens, eds., *The Oxford Handbook of Transformations of the State*. Oxford: Oxford University Press, pp. 691–713.

Evans, P. & Stephens, J. D. (1988). Studying development since the sixties: The emergence of a new comparative political economy. *Theory and Society*, 17(5), 713–45.

Feenstra, R. & Wei, S.-J., eds. (2010). *China's Growing Role in World Trade*. Chicago: The University of Chicago Press.

Feenstra, R. C. & Wei, S.-J., eds., (2010). *China's Growing Role in World Trade*. Washington, DC: National Bureau of Economic Research.

Fine, B. (2013). Beyond the developmental state: An introduction. In B. Fine, J. Saraswati and D. Tavasci, eds., *Beyond the Developmental State: Industrial Policy into the Twenty-first Century*. London: Pluto Press, pp. 1–32.

Fine, B. & Pollen, G. (2018). The developmental state paradigm in an age of financialization. In G. H. Fagan and R. Munck, eds., *Handbook on Development and Social Change*. Cheltenham: Edward Elgar, pp. 211–27.

Fishwick, A. (2019). Labour control and developmental state theory: A new perspective on import-substitution industrialization in Latin America. *Development and Change*, 50(3), 655–78.

Frankel, J. A. (2010). The natural resource curse: A survey. *Working Paper*, No 15836, National Bureau of Economic Research.

Friel, D. (2024). *The Future of Work in Diverse Economic Systems*. Cambridge: Cambridge University Press.

Fukuoka, Y. (2012). Oligarchy and democracy in post-Suharto Indonesia. *Political Studies Review*, 11(1), 52–64.

Funke, M., Schularick, M. and Trebesch, C. (2016). Going to extremes: Politics after financial crises, 1870–2014. *European Economic Review*, 88, 227–60.

Gainsborough, M. (2017). The Myth of a centralised socialist state in Vietnam: What kind of a myth? *Journal of Current Southeast Asian Affairs*, 36(3), 119–43.

Gallagher, M. & Prates, D. M. (2016). New developmentalism versus the financialization of the resource curse. In B. R. Schneider, ed., *New Order and Progress: Development and Democracy in Brazil*. Oxford: Oxford University Press, 78–104.

Gellert, P. K. (2019). Neoliberalism and altered state developmentalism in the twenty-first century extractive regime of Indonesia. *Globalizations*, 16(6), 894–918.

Gereffi, G. (2018). *Global Value Chains and Development: Redefining the Contours of 21st Century Capitalism*. Cambridge: Cambridge University Press.

Gertler, M. (2003). The spatial life of things: the real world of practice within the global firm. In J. Peck and H. Yeung, eds., *Remaking the Global Economy*. London: Sage, pp. 101–113.

Gomes, A. d. P. & ten Brink, T. (2023). *A Chinese Bureaucracy for Innovation-Driven Development?* Cambridge: Cambridge University Press.

Green, J. (2022). Comparative capitalisms in the Anthropocene: a research agenda for green transition. *New Political Economy*, 28(3), 329–46.

Greif, A. (2006). *Institutions and the Path to the Modern Economy: Lessons from Medieval Trade*. Cambridge: Cambridge University Press.

Güngen, A. R. & Akcay, Ü. (2024). Growth models, growth strategies, and power blocs in Turkey and Egypt in the twenty-first century. *European Journal of Economics and Economic Policies: Intervention*, 21(1), 151–71.

Hadiz, V. R. & Robison, R. (2013). The political economy of oligarchy and the reorganization of power in Indonesia. *Indonesia*, 96, 35–57.

Haggard, S. (2019). *Developmental States*. Cambridge: Cambridge University Press.

Haggard, S., Kim, B. & Moon, C. (1991). The transition to export-led growth in South Korea: 1954–1966. *The Journal of Asian Studies*, 50(4), 850–73.

Hall, P. A. (2018). Varieties of capitalism in light of the Euro crisis. *Journal of European Public Policy*, 25, 7–30.

Hall, P. A. & Soskice, D., eds., (2001). *Varieties of Capitalism: The Institutional Foundations of Comparative Advantage*. Oxford: Oxford University Press

Hassel, A. & Palier, B. (2021). Tracking the transformation of growth regimes in advanced capitalist economies. In A. Hassel and B. Palier, eds., *Growth and Welfare in Advanced Capitalist Economies: How Have Growth Regimes Evolved?* Oxford: Oxford University Press, pp. 3–56.

Hassel, A. & Palier, B., (2023). Same trend, different paths: Growth and welfare regimes across time and space. *Annual Review of Political Science*, 26, 347–68.

Hausmann, R., Hwang, J. & Rodrik, D. (2007). What you export matters. *Journal of Economic Growth*, 12, 1–25.

Hay, C. (2020). Does capitalism (still) come in varieties? *Review of International Political Economy*, 27(2), 302–19.

Hein, E. (2014). *Distribution and Growth after Keynes: A Post-Keynesian Guide*. Cheltenham: Edward Elgar.

Hein, E., Paternesi Meloni, W. & Tridico, P. (2021). Welfare models and demand-led growth regimes before and after the financial and economic crisis. *Review of International Political Economy*, 28(5), 1196–223.

Hilmawan, R. & Clark, J. (2019). An investigation of the resource curse in Indonesia. *Resources Policy*, 64, 101483.

Holland, M. (2019). Fiscal crisis in Brazil: Causes and remedy. *Brazilian Journal of Political Economy*, 39(1), 88–107.

Hope, D. & Soskice, D. (2016). Growth models, varieties of capitalism, and macroeconomics. *Politics and Society*, 44(2), 209–26.

Hughes, R. (1998). Considering the vignette technique and its application to a study of drug injecting and HIV risk and safer behaviour. *Sociology of Health & Illness*, 20(3), 381–400.

Ianni, J. M. (2024). Macroeconomic policy regimes and demand and growth regimes in emerging market economies: The case of Argentina. *European Journal of Economics and Economic Policies*, 21(1), 90–112.

IMF, International Monetary Fund. (2012). *World Economic Outlook: Growth Resuming, Dangers Remain*. April. Washington, DC: International Monetary Fund.

Ince, O. U. (2024). Saving capitalism from empire: Uses of colonial history in new institutional economics. *International Relations*, 38(4), 598–614.

Irwin, D. A. (2021). The rise and fall of import substitution. *World Development*, 139, 105306.

Isaacs, G. & Kaltenbrunner, A. (2018). Financialization and liberalization: South Africa's new forms of external vulnerability. *Competition & Change*, 22(4), 437–63.

Jepson, N. (2020). *In China's Wake: How the Commodity Boom Transformed Development Strategies in the Global South*. New York, NY: Columbia University Press.

Jiang, J. (2018). Making bureaucracy work: patronage networks, performance incentives, and economic development in China. *American Journal of Political Science*, 62(4), 982–99.

Johnson, C. (1982). *MITI and the Japanese Miracle: The Growth of Industrial Policy, 1925–1975*. Stanford, CA: Stanford University Press.

Johnson, P. & Papageorgiou, C. (2020). What remains of cross-country convergence? *Journal of Economic Literature*, 58(1), 129–75.

Johnston, A. & Regan, A. (2016). European monetary integration and the incompatibility of national varieties of capitalism. *Journal of Common Market Studies*, 54(2), 318–36.

Jones, B. F. & Olken, B. A. (2008). The anatomy of start-stop growth. *The Review of Economics and Statistics*, 90(3), 582–87.

Jones, C., & Vollrath, D. (2013). *Introduction to Economic Growth*, 3rd ed. London: W.W. Norton.

Jungmann, B. (2023). Growth drivers in emerging capitalist economies: building blocks for a post-Keynesian analysis and an empirical exploration of the years before and after the global financial crisis. *Review of Evolutionary Political Economy*, 4, 349–86.

Kaczmarczyk, P. (2020). Growth models and the footprint of transnational capital. *Maxpo Discussion Paper*, No 20/2. Max Planck Sciences Po Center on Coping with Instability in Market Societies, Paris.

Kalanta, M. (2024). Growth model change in emerging economies: sectorial loci of growth. *Socio-Economic Review*, 22(4), 1783–809.

Kanchoochat, V., Aiyara, T. & Ngamarunchot, B. (2021). Sick tiger: Social conflict, state–business relations and exclusive growth in Thailand. *Journal of Contemporary Asia*, 51(5), 737–58.

Kar, S., Pritchett, L., Raihan, S. & Sen, K. 2013. Looking for a break: Identifying transitions in growth regimes. *Journal of Macroeconomics*, 38 (Part B), 151–66.

Kara, A. H. (2012). Monetary Policy in Turkey After the Global Crisis. *Working Paper No. 12/17*. Ankara: Central Bank of the Republic of Turkey.

Karwowski, E. (2015). The finance-mining nexus in South Africa: How mining companies use the South African equity markets to speculate. *Journal of South African Studies*, 41(1), 9–28.

Karwowski, E. (2018). Corporate financialization in South Africa: from investment strike to housing bubble. *Competition & Change*, 22(4), 413–36.

Kelsall, T., Schulz, N., Ferguson, W. D., et al. (2022). *Political Settlements and Development: Theory, Evidence, Implications*. Oxford: Oxford University Press.

Khan, M. (2000). Rents, efficiency and growth. In M. H. Khan and K. S. Jomo, eds., *Rents, Rent-seeking and Economic Development: Theory and Evidence in Asia*. Cambridge: Cambridge University Press, pp. 21–69.

Khan, M. H. (2010). Political settlements and the governance of growth-enhancing institutions. Draft Paper in Research Paper Series on "Growth-Enhancing Governance." https://eprints.soas.ac.uk/9968/1/Political_Settlements_internet.pdf [accessed April 4, 2025].

Kiran, J. (2018). Expanding the framework of the varieties of capitalism: Turkey as a hierarchical market economy. *Journal of Eurasian Studies*, 9(1), 42–51.

Klingler-Vidra, R. & Wade, R. (2020). Science and technology policies and the middle-income trap: Lessons from Vietnam. *Journal of Development Studies*, 56(4), 717–31.

Koepke, R. (2019). What drives capital flows to emerging markets? A survey of the empirical literature. *Journal of Economic Surveys*, 33(2), 516–540.

Kohler, K. (2022). Capital flows and geographically uneven economic dynamics: A monetary perspective. *Environment and Planning A: Economy and Space*, 54(8), 1510–31.

Kohler, K. & Stockhammer, E. (2022). Growing differently? Financial cycles, austerity, and competitiveness in growth models since the global financial crisis. *Review of International Political Economy*, 29(4), 1314–41.

Kohli, A. (2004). *State-Directed Development: Political Power and Industrialization in the Global Periphery*. Cambridge: Cambridge University Press.

Kongkirati, P. (2016). Thailand's failed 2014 election: The anti-election movement, violence and democratic breakdown. *Journal of Contemporary Asia*, 46(3), 467–85.

Kutlay, M. (2020). The politics of state capitalism in a post-liberal international order: The case of Turkey. *Third World Quarterly*, 41(2), 683–706.

Kvangraven, I. H. (2021). Beyond the Stereotype: Restating the Relevance of the Dependency Research Programme. *Development and Change*, 52(1), 76–112.

Kvangraven, I. H., Koddenbrock, K. & Sylla, N. S. (2021). Financial subordination and uneven financialization in 21st century Africa. *Community Development Journal*, 56(1), 119–40.

Lapavitsas, C. & Soydan, A. (2022). Financialisation in developing countries: Approaches, concepts, and metrics. *International Review of Applied Economics*, 36(3), 424–47.

Lee, K. (2013). *Schumpeterian Analysis of Economic Catch-up: Knowledge, Path-Creation, and the Middle-Income Trap*. Cambridge: Cambridge University Press.

Lewis, A. W. (1954). Economic development with unlimited supplies of labour. *The Manchester School*, 22(2), 139–91.

Lim, G. (2021). *The Political Economy of Growth in Vietnam: Between States and Markets*. New York, NY: Routledge.

Liu, Z. (2008). Foreign direct investment and technology spillovers: Theory and evidence. *Journal of Development Economics*, 85, 176–93.

London, J. D. (2022). The communist party of Vietnam: Consolidating market-Leninism. In J. D. London, ed., *Routledge Handbook of Contemporary Vietnam*. London: Routledge, pp. 21–47.

Lorch, J. (2021). Elite capture, civil society and democratic backsliding in Bangladesh, Thailand and the Philippines. *Democratization*, 28(1), 81–102.

Madariaga, A. & Palestini, S., eds., (2021). *Dependent Capitalisms in Contemporary Latin America and Europe*. Cham: Cambridge Macmillan.

Madra, Y. M., Bengi, A. & Adaman, F. (2025). Decolonizing development economics: A critique of the late neoclassical reason. *World Development*, 188, 106875.

Malesky, E. & London, J. (2014). The political economy of development in China and Vietnam. *Annual Review of Political Science*, 17, 395–419.

Marglin, S. A. & Schor, J., eds., (1991). *The Golden Age of Capitalism: Reinterpreting the Postwar Experience*. Oxford: Oxford University Press.

Marques, P. R. (2025). Unraveling growth models in peripheral economies: Kalecki's political business cycle and Brazil's "pink tide" experience. *Review of Political Economy*, 37(3), 1138–63.

Masi, T., Savoia, A. & Sen, K. (2024). Is there a fiscal resource curse? Resource rents, fiscal capacity and political institutions in developing economies. *World Development*, 177, 106532.

Maxfield, S. & Schneider, B. R. (1997). Business, the state, and economic performance in developing countries. In B. R. Schneider and S. Maxfield, eds., *Business and the State in Developing Countries*. Ithaca, NY: Cornell University Press, pp. 3–35.

May, C. (2020). Globalizing state capitalism? Selective internationalization of MNCs from emerging economies. In J. Mikler and K. Ronit, eds., *MNCs in Global Politics: Pathways of Influence*. Cheltenham: Edward Elgar, pp. 30–46.

May, C., Mertens, D., Nölke, A. & Schedelik, M. (2024). *Political Economy: Comparative, International, and Historical Perspectives*. Cham: Springer.

May, C., Nölke, A. & Schedelik, M. (2024). Growth models and social blocs: Taking Gramsci seriously. *Competition & Change*, 29(3–4), 334–351.

Mazzucato, M. (2013). *The Entrepreneurial State: Debunking Public vs. Private Sector Myths*. London: Anthem Press.

Mazzucato, M. (2023). Financing the sustainable development goals through mission-oriented development banks. *UN DESA Policy Brief* Special issue, September. New York, NY: UN Department of Economic and Social Affairs.

Mertens, D., Nölke, A., May, C., et al. (2022). Moving the center: Adapting the toolbox of growth model research to emerging capitalist economies. *IPE Working Paper*, No 188/2022, Berlin: Institute for International Political Economy.

Merton, R. K. (1968). *Social Theory and Social Structure*. New York, NY: The Free Press.

Mesquita Moreira, M., Rodríguez Chatruc, M., Lage de Sousa, F. & Merchán, F. (2020). Trade, productivity, innovation, and employment: Lessons from the impact of Chinese competition on manufacturing in Brazil. *IDB Publications (Working Papers)* 10517, Inter-American Development Bank.

Migdal, J. (2001). *State in Society. Studying How States and Societies Transform and Constitute One Another*. Cambridge: Cambridge University Press.

Miranda-Agrippino, S. & Rey, H. (2022). The global financial cycle. In G. Gopinath, E. Helpman and K. Rogoff, eds., *Handbook of International Economics*, Vol. 6. Amsterdam: North Holland, pp. 1–43.

Moehlecke, C., Thrall, C. & Wellhausen, C. L. (2023). Global value chains as a constraint on sovereignty: Evidence from investor–state dispute settlement. *International Studies Quarterly*, 67(1), 1–16.

Molina, L. & Viani, F. (2019). Capital flows to emerging economies: Recent developments and drivers. *Economic Bulletin/Banco de España*, 2/2019, 1–8

Morgan, G., Doering, H. & Gomes, M. (2021). Extending varieties of capitalism to emerging economies: what can we learn from Brazil? *New Political Economy*, 26(4), 540–53.

Naseemullah, A. (2023). The political economy of national development: A research agenda after neoliberal reform? *World Development*, 168, 106269.

Natanael, Y. (2025). Is less commodity dependence better for economic equality, economic growth, and human development? *Global Journal of Emerging Market Economies*, 17(2), 199–221.

Naqvi, N. (2023). Economic crisis, global financial cycles and state control of finance: Public development banking in Brazil and South Africa. *European Journal of International Relations*, 29(2), 283–318.

Nidhiprabha, B. (2017). The rise and fall of Thailand's export-oriented industries. *Asian Economic Papers*, 16(3), 128–50.

Nkurunziza, J., Tsowou, K. & Cazzaniga, S. (2017). Commodity dependence and human development. *African Development Review* 29(S1), 27–41.

Ngo, C. & Tarko, V. (2018). Economic development in a rent-seeking society: Socialism, state capitalism and crony capitalism in Vietnam. *Canadian Journal of Development Studies*, 39(4), 481–99.

Nguyen, T. P. (2014). Business associations and the politics of contained participation in Vietnam. *Australian Journal of Political Science*, 49(2), 334–49.

Nölke, A. (2021). In search of institutional complementarities: Comparative capitalism and economic policy reform. *Journal of Economic Policy Reform*, 24(4), 405–12.

Nölke, A. & Vliegenthart, A. (2009). Enlarging the varieties of capitalism: The emergence of dependent market economies in East Central Europe. *World Politics*, 61(4), 670–702.

Nölke, A., ten Brink, T., May, C. & Claar, S. (2020). *State-permeated Capitalism in Large Emerging Economies*. New York, NY: Routledge.

Nölke, A., May, C., Mertens, D. & Schedelik, M. (2022). Elephant limps, but jaguar stumbles: Unpacking the divergence of state capitalism in Brazil and India through theories of capitalist diversity. *Competition & Change*, 26(3–4), 311–33.

North, D. (1995). The new institutional economics and third world development. In J. Harris, J. Hunter and C. Lewis, eds., *The New Institutional Economics and Third World Development*. New York, NY: Routledge, pp. 17–26.

Nugent, J. B. (2023). A new institutional perspective on business associations: Filling a gap between firms and states in the dynamic analysis of Richard Day. *Journal of Economic Behavior & Organization*, 211, 49–59.

OECD, Organisation for Economic Co-operation and Development. (2018a). Indonesia. *OECD Economic Outlook 2018*, No. 2. Paris.

OECD, Organisation for Economic Co-operation and Development. (2018b). *OECD Investment Policy Reviews*: *Viet Nam*, Paris.

Owen, E. (2018). Foreign direct investment and elections: the impact of greenfield FDI on incumbent party reelection in Brazil. *Comparative Political Studies*, 52(4), 613–45.

Özel, I. (2015). *State–Business Alliances and Economic Development Turkey, Mexico and North Africa*. London: Routledge.

Pandya, S. S. (2016). Political economy of foreign direct investment: Globalized production in the twenty-first century. *Annual Review of Political Science*, 19, 455–75.

Passos, N. & Morlin, G. S. (2022). Growth models and comparative political economy in Latin America. *Revue de la régulation*, 33(2), 1–23.

Pepinsky, T. B. (2013). The domestic politics of financial internationalization in the developing world. *Review of International Political Economy*, 20(4), 848–89.

Pepinsky, T. B. (2014). Pluralism and political conflict in Indonesia. In M. Ford and T. B. Pepinsky, eds., *Beyond Oligarchy: Wealth, Power, and Contemporary Indonesian Politics*. Ithaca, NY: Cornell University Press, pp. 79–98.

Petry, J. & Nölke, A. (2025). Introduction: subordination, statecraft, and comparative capitalism. In J. Petry and A. Nölke, eds., *State, Capitalism, and Finance in Emerging Markets*. Bristol: Bristol University Press, pp. 3–21.

Petry, J., Nölke, A. & Koddenbrock, K. (2024). State capitalism and capital markets: Comparing securities exchanges in emerging markets. *Environment and Planning A: Economy and Space*, 55(1), 143–64.

Picot, G. (2021). Cross-national variation in growth models: Three sources of extra demand. In A. Hassel and B. Palier, eds., *Growth and Welfare in Advanced Capitalist Economies: How Have Growth Regimes Evolved?* Oxford: Oxford University Press, pp. 135–60.

Pincus, J. (2023). Contemporary Vietnam: State effectiveness under conditions of commercialization. In J. D. London, ed., *Routledge Handbook of Contemporary Vietnam*. New York, NY: Routledge, pp. 164–83.

Pinto, P. M. & Zhu, B. (2022). Brewing violence: Foreign investment and civil conflict. *Journal of Conflict Resolution*, 66(6), 1010–36.

Pipkin, S. & Fuentes, A. (2017). Spurred to upgrade: A review of triggers and consequences of industrial upgrading in the global value chain literature. *World Development*, 98, 536–54.

Porteux, J. N. & Kim, S. (2023). Delegating violence in democracies: Embedded developmentalism and persistence of labor repression in South Korea. *Japanese Journal of Political Science*, 24(2), 249–69.

Power, T. J. & Rodrigues-Silveira, R. (2019). The political right and party politics. In B. Ames, ed., *Routledge Handbook of Brazilian Politics*. New York, NY: Routledge, pp. 251–68.

Pritchett, L., Sen, K. & Werker, E., eds., (2017). *Deals and Development: The Political Dynamics of Growth Episodes*. Oxford: Oxford University Press.

Qiang, C.-Z., Liu, Y. & Steenbergen, V. (2021). *An Investment Perspective on Global Value Chains*. Washington, DC: World Bank.

Rajah, R. (2018). *Indonesia's Economy: Between Growth and Stability*. Sidney: Lowy Institute.

Reinhart, C. M., Reinhart, V. & Trebesch, C. (2016). Global cylces: Capital flows, commodities, and sovereign defaults, 1815–2015. *American Economic Review*, 106(5), 574–80

Ricz, J. & Schedelik, M. (2023). Brazil's national champions strategy (2007–13): A critical appraisal. *Competition & Change*, online first.

Rodrigue, J.-P. (2024). *The Geography of Transport Systems*, 6th ed. New York, NY: Routledge.

Rodrik, D. (2009). Industrial policy: Don't ask why, ask how. *Middle East Development Journal*, 1(1), 1–29.

Rodrik, D. (2025). *Shared Prosperity in a Fractured World: A New Economics for the Middle Class, the Global Poor, and Our Climate*. Princeton, NJ: Princeton University Press.

Rodrik, D. & Joseph, E. S. (2024). A new growth strategy for developing nations. January 2024. htps://drodrik.scholar.harvard.edu/publications/new-growth-strategy-developing-natons [accessed April 4, 2025].

Rodrik, D., Subramanian, A. & Trebbi, F. (2004). Institutions rule: The primacy of institutions over geography and integration in economic development. *Journal of Economic Growth*, 9, 131–65.

Ross, M. L. (2015). What have we learned about the resource curse? *Annual Review of Political Science*, 18, 239–59.

Rostow, W. W. (1960). *The Stages of Economic Growth: A Non-Communist Manifesto*. Cambridge: Cambridge University Press.

Sayarı, S. (2014). Interdisciplinary approaches to political clientelism and patronage in Turkey. *Turkish Studies*, 15(4), 655–70.

Schedelik, M. (2023). *The Political Economy of Upgrading Regimes: Brazil and Beyond*. New York, NY: Palgrave Macmillan.

Schedelik, M., Nölke, A., Mertens, D. & May, C. (2021). Comparative capitalism, growth models and emerging markets: the development of the field. *New Political Economy*, 26(4), 514–26.

Schedelik, M., Nölke, A., May, C. & Gomes, A. (2023). Dependency revisited: Commodities, commodity-related capital flows and growth models in emerging economies. *European Journal of Economics and Economic Policies: Intervention*, 20(3), 515–38.

Schedelik, M. & Nölke, A. (2025). Peripheral growth models and the global economy: A second image IPE perspective. *MPIfG Discussion Paper* 25/5. Cologne: Max Planck Institute for the Study of Societies.

Scheiring, G. (2020). *The Retreat of Liberal Democracy: Authoritarian Capitalism and the Accumulative State in Hungary*. Houndmills: Palgrave Macmillan.

Schlumberger, O. (2008). Structural reform, economic order, and development: Patrimonial capitalism. *Review of International Political Economy*, 15(4), 622–49.

Schneider, B. R. (2009). Hierarchical market economies and varieties of capitalism in Latin America. *Journal of Latin American Studies*, 41(3), 553–75.

Schneider, B. R. (2013). *Hierarchical Capitalism in Latin America: Business, Labor, and the Challenges of Equitable Development*. Cambridge: Cambridge University Press.

Schröder, M. & Iwasaki, F. (2023). From nickel to electric cars? Indonesia's resource cum automotive industry policy. *Journal of the Asia Pacific Economy*, 29(4), 2065–86.

Schwartz, H. M. & Tranøy, B. S. (2019). Thinking about thinking about comparative political economy: From macro to micro and back. *Politics and Society*, 47(1), 23–54.

Sen, K. (2023). *Varieties of Structural Transformation: Patterns, Determinants, and Consequences*. Cambridge: Cambridge University Press.

Sen, K., Pritchett, L., Kar, S. & Raihan, S. (2018). Democracy versus dictatorship? The political determinants of growth episodes. *Journal of Development Perspectives*, 2(1–2), 3–28.

Sen, K. & Tyce, M. (2019). The elusive quest for high income status – Malaysia and Thailand in the post-crisis years. *Structural Change and Economic Dynamics*, 48, 117–35.

Shonfield, A. (1965). *Modern Capitalism: The Changing Balance of Public and Private Power*. London: Oxford University Press.

Stallings, B. (2022). *Dependency in the Twenty-First Century? The Political Economy of China-Latin America Relations*. Cambridge: Cambridge University Press.

Stiglitz, J. & Lin, J., eds. (2013). *The Industrial Policy Revolution I: The Role of Government beyond Ideology*. New York, NY: Palgrave Macmillan.

Stockhammer, E. (2022). Post-Keynesian macroeconomic foundations for comparative political economy. *Politics and Society*, 50(1), 156–87.

Stockhammer, E. (2023). Macroeconomic ingredients for a growth model analysis for peripheral economies: A post-Keynesian structuralist approach. *New Political Economy*, 28(4), 628–45.

Strange, S. (1996). *Retreat of the State*. Cambridge: Cambridge University Press.

Streeck, W. (2010). E pluribus unum? Varieties and commonalities of capitalism. *MPIfG Discussion Paper* 10/12. Cologne: Max Planck Institute for the Study of Societies.

Swedberg, R. (2018). How to use Max Weber's ideal type in sociological analysis. *Journal of Classical Sociology*, 18(3), 181–96.

Sugiyama, N. B. & Hunter, W. (2013). Whither clientelism? Good governance and Brazil's "Bolsa Família" program. *Comparative Politics*, 46(1), 43–62.

Taylor, M. M. (2020). *Decadent Developmentalism: The Political Economy of Democratic Brazil*. Cambridge: Cambridge University Press.

ten Brink, T. (2019). *China's Capitalism: A Paradoxical Route to Economic Prosperity*. Philadelphia, PA: University of Pennsylvania Press.

Topal, A. (2019). The state, crisis and transformation of small and medium-sized enterprise finance in Turkey. In G. L. Yalman, T. Marois and A. R. Güngen, eds., *The Political Economy of Financial Transformation in Turkey*. New York, NY: Routledge, pp. 221–42.

Toral, G. (2023). How patronage delivers: Political appointments, bureaucratic accountability, and service delivery in Brazil. *American Journal of Political Science*, 68(2), 797–815.

UNCTAD. (2019). *Commodity Dependence: A Twenty-Year Perspective*. Geneva: United Nations Conference on Trade and Development.

UNCTAD. (2021). *Escaping from the Commodity Dependence Trap through Technology and Innovation*. Commodities and Development Report 2021. Geneva: United Nations Conference on Trade and Development.

UNCTAD. (2024). *World Investment Report 2024*. Geneva: United Nations Conference on Trade and Development.

United Nations (2025). Gross domestic product by expenditures at constant prices. National Accounts Statistics: Main Aggregates and Detailed Tables. Washington, DC: https://unstats.un.org/unsd/nationalaccount/madt.asp [accessed April 4, 2025].

Wade, R. (1990). *Governing the Market: Economic Theory and the Role of Government in East Asian Industrialization*. Princeton, NJ: Princeton University Press.

Waldner, D. (1999). *State Building and Late Development*. Ithaca, NY: Cornell University Press.

Wallerstein, I. (1976). *The Modern World-System*. New York, NY: Academic Press.

Wang, S., He, Y. & Song, M. (2021). Global value chains, technological progress, and environmental pollution: Inequality towards developing countries. *Journal of Environmental Management*, 277, 110999.

Wanklin, Linda M. (2025). Growth and emerging economies: The rise of remittances-based growth regimes and transnational skill formation in Kosovo. In A. Hassel and B. Palier, eds., *Growth Strategies and Welfare Reforms: How Nations Cope with Economic Transitions*. Oxford: Oxford University Press, pp. 337–71.

Warburton, E. (2016). Jokowi and the new developmentalism. *Bulletin of Indonesian Economic Studies*, 52(3), 297–320.

Warburton, E. (2017). Resource nationalism in Indonesia: Ownership structures and sectoral variation in mining and palm oil. *Journal of East Asian Studies*, 17(3), 285–312.

Warburton, E. (2018). A new developmentalism in Indonesia? *Journal of South East Asian Economies*, 35(3), 355–68.

Warburton, E. (2023). *Resource Nationalism in Indonesia: Booms, Big Business, and the State*. Ithaca, NY: Cornell University Press.

Weber, M. (1947 [1922]). *Methodology of the Social Sciences*, translated by E. A. Shils & H. A. Finch. Glencoe, IL: Free Press.

Welch, C., Piekkari, R., Plakoyiannaki, E. & Paavilainen-Mäntymäki, E. (2011). Theorising from case studies: Towards a pluralist future for international business research. *Journal of International Business Studies*, 42, 740–62.

Winanti, P. S. & Diprose, R. (2020). Reordering the extractive political settlement: Resource nationalism, domestic ownership and transnational bargains in Indonesia. *The Extractive Industries and Society*, 7(4), 1534–46.

Witt, M. A. & Redding, G. (2013). Asian business systems: Institutional comparison, clusters and implications for Varieties of Capitalism and business systems theory. *Socio-Economic Review*, 11(2), 265–300.

Wood, G. & Schnyder, G. (2021). Intro: Comparative capitalism research in emerging markets – a new generation. *New Political Economy*, 26(4), 509–13.

World Bank. (1993). *The East Asian Miracle: Economic Growth and Public Policy*. Oxford: Oxford University Press.

World Bank. (2018). *Commodity Markets Outlook*, October 2018. Washington, DC: World Bank.

World Bank. (2025). GDP growth (annual %). World development indicators. Washington, DC. https://data.worldbank.org/indicator/NY.GDP.MKTP.KD.ZG [accessed April 4, 2025].

Yavuz, D. (2010). Testing large business's commitment to democracy: Business organizations and the secular–Muslim conflict in Turkey. *Government and Opposition*, 45(1), 73–92.

Zayim, A. (2022). Financialized growth and the structural power of finance: Turkey's debt-led growth regime and policy response after the crisis. *Politics & Society*, 50(4), 543–70.

Acknowledgments

This work was supported by the German Research Foundation under grant numbers 218893009 and 396568804. Parts of Sections 1 to 3 rely on Mertens et al. (2022), and parts of Section 4 rely on Schedelik and Nölke (2025). We want to thank Fulya Apaydin, Sonja Avlijaš, Benjamin Jungmann, Katharina Kuhn, Aila Trasi, Pedro Mendes Loureiro, and two anonymous reviewers for invaluable comments and suggestions on earlier versions of the manuscript.

Cambridge Elements

Development Economics

Series Editor-in-Chief
Kunal Sen
UNU-WIDER and University of Manchester

Kunal Sen, UNU-WIDER Director, is Editor-in-Chief of the Cambridge Elements in Development Economics series. Professor Sen has over three decades of experience in academic and applied development economics research, and has carried out extensive work on international finance, the political economy of inclusive growth, the dynamics of poverty, social exclusion, female labour force participation, and the informal sector in developing economies. His research has focused on India, East Asia, and sub-Saharan Africa.

In addition to his work as Professor of Development Economics at the University of Manchester, Kunal has been the Joint Research Director of the Effective States and Inclusive Development (ESID) Research Centre, and a Research Fellow at the Institute for Labor Economics (IZA). He has also served in advisory roles with national governments and bilateral and multilateral development agencies, including the UK's Department for International Development, Asian Development Bank, and the International Development Research Centre.

Thematic Editors
Tony Addison
University of Copenhagen and UNU-WIDER

Tony Addison is a Professor of Economics in the University of Copenhagen's Development Economics Research Group. He is also a Non-Resident Senior Research Fellow at UNU-WIDER, Helsinki, where he was previously the Chief Economist-Deputy Director. In addition, he is Professor of Development Studies at the University of Manchester. His research interests focus on the extractive industries, energy transition, and macroeconomic policy for development.

Chris Barrett
SC Johnson College of Business, Cornell University

Chris Barrett is an agricultural and development economist at Cornell University. He is the Stephen B. and Janice G. Ashley Professor of Applied Economics and Management and International Professor of Agriculture at the Charles H. Dyson School of Applied Economics and Management. He is also an elected Fellow of the American Association for the Advancement of Science, the Agricultural and Applied Economics Association, and the African Association of Agricultural Economists.

Carlos Gradín
University of Vigo

Carlos Gradín is a professor of applied economics at the University of Vigo. His main research interest is the study of inequalities, with special attention to those that exist between population groups (e.g., by race or sex). His publications have contributed to improving the empirical evidence in developing and developed countries, as well as globally, and to improving the available data and methods used.

Rachel M. Gisselquist
UNU-WIDER

Rachel M. Gisselquist is a Senior Research Fellow and member of the Senior Management Team of UNU-WIDER. She specializes in the comparative politics of developing countries, with particular attention to issues of inequality, ethnic and identity politics, foreign aid and state building, democracy and governance, and sub-Saharan African politics. Dr Gisselquist has edited a dozen collections in these areas, and her articles are published in a range of leading journals.

Shareen Joshi
Georgetown University

Shareen Joshi is an Associate Professor of International Development at Georgetown University's School of Foreign Service in the United States. Her research focuses on issues of inequality, human capital investment, and grassroots collective action in South Asia. Her work has been published in the fields of development economics, population studies, environmental studies, and gender studies.

Patricia Justino
UNU-WIDER and IDS – UK

Patricia Justino is a Senior Research Fellow at UNU-WIDER and Professorial Fellow at the Institute of Development Studies (IDS) (on leave). Her research focuses on the relationship between political violence, governance, and development outcomes. She has published widely in the fields of development economics and political economy and is the co-founder and co-director of the Households in Conflict Network (HiCN).

Marinella Leone
University of Pavia

Marinella Leone is an assistant professor at the Department of Economics and Management, University of Pavia, Italy. She is an applied development economist. Her more recent research focuses on the study of early child development parenting programmes, on education, and gender-based violence. In previous research, she investigated the short-, long-term, and intergenerational impact of conflicts on health, education, and domestic violence. She has published in top journals in economics and development economics.

Jukka Pirttilä
University of Helsinki and UNU-WIDER

Jukka Pirttilä is Professor of Public Economics at the University of Helsinki and VATT Institute for Economic Research. He is also a Non-Resident Senior Research Fellow at UNU-WIDER. His research focuses on tax policy, especially for developing countries. He is a co-principal investigator at the Finnish Centre of Excellence in Tax Systems Research.

Andy Sumner
King's College London and UNU-WIDER

Andy Sumner is Professor of International Development at King's College London; a Non-Resident Senior Fellow at UNU-WIDER and a Fellow of the Academy of Social Sciences. He has published extensively in the areas of poverty, inequality, and economic development.

About the Series

Cambridge Elements in Development Economics is led by UNU-WIDER in partnership with Cambridge University Press. The series publishes authoritative studies on important topics in the field covering both micro and macro aspects of development economics.

United Nations University World Institute for Development Economics Research

United Nations University World Institute for Development Economics Research (UNU-WIDER) provides economic analysis and policy advice aiming to promote sustainable and equitable development for all. The institute began operations in 1985 in Helsinki, Finland, as the first research centre of the United Nations University. Today, it is one of the world's leading development economics think tanks, working closely with a vast network of academic researchers and policy makers, mostly based in the Global South.

Cambridge Elements

Development Economics

Elements in the Series

Economic Transformation and Income Distribution in China over Three Decades
Cai Meng, Bjorn Gustafsson and John Knight

Chilean Economic Development under Neoliberalism: Structural Transformation, High Inequality and Environmental Fragility
Andrés Solimano and Gabriela Zapata-Román

Hierarchy of Needs and the Measurement of Poverty and Standards of Living
Joseph Deutsch and Jacques Silber

New Structural Financial Economics: A Framework for Rethinking the Role of Finance in Serving the Real Economy
Justin Yifu Lin, Jiajun Xu, Zirong Yang and Yilin Zhang

Knowledge and Global Inequality Since 1800: Interrogating the Present as History
Dev Nathan

Survival of the Greenest: Economic Transformation in a Climate-conscious World
Amir Lebdioui

Escaping Poverty Traps and Unlocking Prosperity in the Face of Climate Risk: Lessons from Index-Based Livestock Insurance
Nathaniel D. Jensen, Francesco P. Fava, Andrew G. Mude, Christopher B. Barrett, Brenda Wandera-Gache, Anton Vrieling, Masresha Taye, Kazushi Takahashi, Felix Lung, Munenobu Ikegami, Polly Ericksen, Philemon Chelanga, Sommarat Chantarat, Michael Carter, Hassan Bashir, and Rupsha Banerjee

Financing for Development: The Global Agenda
José Antonio Ocampo

Poverty in Latin America: Feelings/Perceptions vs Material Conditions
Verónica Amarante, Maira Colacce, and Federico Scalese

Trade in Tasks: A New Perspective to International Trade, Structural Change, and Economic Development
Gaaitzen J. de Vries and Marcel P. Timmer

Developmental Dilemmas: The Role of Power and Agency
William D. Ferguson

Varieties of Peripheral Growth Models: Towards a New Comparative Political Economy of Development
Michael Schedelik, Christian May, Andreas Nölke, Daniel Mertens, Alexandre De Podestá Gomes and Tobias ten Brink

A full series listing is available at: www.cambridge.org/CEDE

For EU product safety concerns, contact us at Calle de José Abascal, 56–1°,
28003 Madrid, Spain or eugpsr@cambridge.org.

www.ingramcontent.com/pod-product-compliance
Ingram Content Group UK Ltd.
Pitfield, Milton Keynes, MK11 3LW, UK
UKHW022311090326
468823UK00020B/1649